# White Witchcraft vs Dark Psychology

Selena Blackwood

Copyright © 2025 by Selena Blackwood

All rights reserved.

No portion of this book may be reproduced in any form without written permission from the publisher or author, except as permitted by U.S. copyright law.

# Contents

| | |
|---|---|
| Introduction | 1 |
| 1. Foundations of White Witchcraft and Dark Psychology | 5 |
| 2. Recognizing Manipulation and Protective Rituals | 21 |
| 3. Practical Applications of Witchcraft and Psychology | 37 |
| 4. Emotional Healing and Recovery | 52 |
| 5. Ethical Considerations and Responsible Practice | 67 |
| 6. Comprehensive Self-Improvement and Growth | 83 |
| 7. Advanced Techniques and Personal Empowerment | 96 |
| 8. Connecting with Supportive Communities | 110 |
| 9. Conclusion | 127 |
| A Note from Selena | 130 |
| References | 132 |

# Introduction

## WHITE WITCH CRAFT VS DARK PSYCHOLOGY: LEARN TO PROTECT AGAINST MANIPULATION AND DARK ENERGY USING ANCIENT MAGICAL KNOWLEDGE AND MODERN PSYCHOLOGY

*Light and shadows reflect the eternal struggle between white witchcraft and dark psychology. It is a dance as old as time itself, where forces of light strive to protect and heal, while darker elements seek to manipulate and control. This book is born from that struggle, a guide to help you navigate the unseen influences that shape our lives.*

Hi, I'm Selena. I've always been drawn to exploring ideas that go beyond what we're typically taught in school or see on TV. Over the years, I've discovered a unique approach that combines ancient wisdom with modern psychological insights. This fusion has become a powerful toolkit for personal empowerment and self-protection, and I'm excited to share it with you.

Dark Psychology, in my opinion, has existed as long as humans have communicated. From the earliest days, there has been a desire to influence, whether to claim a larger share of the mammoth meat, gain more power, or rise to the position of tribal leader. The methods may have evolved, but the core motivation remains the same: to gain an advantage, often at someone else's expense.

***

In more recent times, humans have given these practices specific names, leading us into the worlds of witchcraft and, later, psychology. I came to realize how deeply connected these two areas are. Practitioners of what we now call dark psychology—long before it had a formal name—used their understanding of human behavior and communication to manipulate and consolidate power. To deflect attention from their own actions, they often needed a scapegoat. In my view, this is where the witch hunts of medieval times found their roots.

Witchcraft was often, though not always, associated with women. These women already faced significant societal challenges, as men—whether fathers, husbands, or other authorities—essentially controlled their lives. Many of them were healers and midwives, possessing knowledge of herbs and remedies passed down through generations. They became easy targets. Blaming societal disturbances on these "witches" conveniently distracted from the larger, more calculated manipulations happening in the background.

On a personal note, my Great Aunt Liesel taught me about herbs, teas, and healing plants from an early age. Sadly, after her passing, her diaries, books, and journals were destroyed. Despite my grandmother and me pleading to preserve them, her children chose otherwise. Could this hint at the complexities of human behavior and the subtle workings of dark psychology?

But I digress. I hope you enjoy this book, as it explores a topic I am deeply passionate about—one I've encountered firsthand in my career as an executive in high-level government roles. And no, I'm not joking! While there was no overt witchcraft, I certainly witnessed the art of dark psychology in action. Interestingly, in many government offices I visited, I saw crystals and talismans from various cultures adorning desks. What does that say about us, I wonder?

***

Let's get into it now;

White witchcraft is the practice of using magic for positive and protective purposes. It is about healing, harmony, and strengthening the spirit. It draws from ancient traditions and honors the natural rhythms of the world.

Dark psychology, on the other hand, is the art of manipulation and control. It exploits the mind's vulnerabilities, using deceit and coercion to achieve selfish ends. Understanding these two forces is essential in a world where manipulation is becoming more sophisticated and pervasive every day.

***

This book is important because it addresses a growing need. In today's world, the threat of manipulation is everywhere. Social media, advertising, and even personal relationships can become arenas for dark psychological tactics. By integrating the wisdom of white witchcraft with modern psychology, this book offers a unique solution. It empowers you with both historical knowledge and contemporary techniques to guard against these hidden influences.

My vision for this book is to guide you through the intricate nuances of these two forces. You will learn to recognize manipulation and protect yourself using both the practices of the wise old woman and the insights of modern psychology. Each chapter is structured to address a specific pain point, providing solutions through the lens of both witchcraft and psychology. This dual approach ensures a comprehensive understanding and practical application.

What sets this book apart is its unique proposition. It combines magical and psychological tools in a way that is both practical and accessible. This approach provides a guide that is equipping you with the skills needed for self-protection and personal growth.

Throughout this book you will gain practical techniques to safeguard and a deeper understanding of manipulation tactics. You will discover how to enhance your own sense of empowerment. Eventually you will be equipped with the knowledge and tools to protect and enrich your life in ways you may not have thought possible.

The knowledge and tools provided here will empower you to protect yourself and enhance your life. Together, let us navigate the interaction of light and shadow, and emerge stronger and wiser for it.

# Foundations of White Witchcraft and Dark Psychology

What makes most of us feel calm and relaxed? Walking through a park, a forest or walking along a beach. That inexplicable serenity is not just our imagination; it's a glimpse into the world of energy that permeates all things. Energy, both seen and unseen, influences our lives more than we might realize. In this chapter, let's explore the foundations of white witchcraft, a tradition rooted in harnessing positive energies for healing and protection. At the same time, we'll touch on the darker arts of psychology, which can manipulate and control. This duality presents a powerful contrast: white magic's benevolence versus dark psychology's shadowy undercurrents. Understanding this balance is essential as we learn to protect from manipulation in a world filled with subtle influences.

## 1.1 The Essence of White Witchcraft

White witchcraft, often misunderstood, is a practice steeped in benevolence and ancient wisdom. At its core, it is about harnessing the positive energies that exist in the world to heal, protect, and uplift. The roots of white witchcraft stretch back to the earliest human civilizations, where rituals and spells were deeply woven into daily life. These practices, as ancient as Paleolithic religion, were integral to survival and well-being, focusing on fertility, health, and prosperity. Historically, practitioners of white magic were revered as wise men and women, healers who used their knowledge to bless and protect their communities. They chanted incantations, crafted charms, and whispered prayers, all aimed at invoking the forces of nature for the greater good.

White witchcraft stands distinct from other forms, like black magic, which is often associated with harmful intent and personal gain. While black magic seeks to dominate and control, white witchcraft operates within an ethical framework that emphasizes the principle of doing no harm. Its practitioners adhere to a code that respects the free will of others, aiming to enhance life rather than diminish it. This ethical stance aligns with the broader moral compass that guides white magic, making it a force for good in a world where intentions can often be murky. The difference lies not just in the spells cast but in the heart and intent behind them.

In today's world, white witchcraft has evolved, embracing modern tools and technologies while staying true to its fundamental principles. New-age spirituality has infused it with contemporary influences, allowing it to adapt and thrive. Today, practitioners might use digital platforms to share rituals or employ apps to track lunar phases. Despite these innovations, the essence remains unchanged: to channel the earth's energies for healing and protection. Incorporating crystals, herbs, and even guided meditations into rituals reflects this evolution, blending age-old practices with the modern quest for mindfulness and balance.

White witchcraft plays a vital role in self-protection, offering tools to shield against negative influences that can pervade our lives. Defensive spells, for instance, are crafted to guard against unwanted energies, creating a barrier that repels harm. These spells can be simple, like a mantra repeated in meditation, or more complex, involving the creation of protective circles. Talismans, too, hold significant power; objects imbued with intention and energy serve as constant guardians. Whether worn on the body or placed in your home, they act as anchors of positive energy, helping to maintain balance and security.

The practice of white witchcraft invites you to explore a world where the mystical becomes practical, where ancient wisdom meets modern life. It encourages self-awareness and empowerment, offering a path to navigate life's challenges with grace and strength. Understanding the principles of white magic provides you with tools for protection and personal growth, tapping into a tradition that has healed and nurtured for centuries. As you become more in tune with this practice, consider how its principles might enhance your life, providing you with a sense of peace and a shield against the world's darker influences.

## 1.2 Unveiling Dark Psychology

Dark psychology is a fascinating yet unsettling field that explores the depths of manipulation and control. It is the study of the darker aspects of human behavior, those murky tactics used to influence and manipulate others for personal gain. At its core, dark psychology examines how individuals use psychological techniques to control others, often without their knowledge. This manipulation can take many forms, from subtle persuasion to outright coercion. Techniques such as gaslighting and emotional blackmail play significant roles, preying on the vulnerabilities of the human psyche. These tactics operate in the shadows of interpersonal relationships, often going unnoticed until the damage is already done.

Pivotal figures and groundbreaking studies mark the journey of dark psychology through history. Sigmund Freud, a towering figure in psychology, laid the groundwork by exploring the unconscious mind and its powerful influence on behavior. His theories on defense mechanisms and the psyche's hidden desires have provided a foundation for understanding manipulation's roots. Decades later, Stanley Milgram's obedience experiments further illuminated the dark corners of human behavior. Conducted in the 1960s, Milgram's research revealed a disturbing tendency for individuals to obey authority figures, even when such obedience conflicts with personal morals. Participants, believing they were part of a learning study, were instructed to deliver electric shocks to a "learner" (an actor) for wrong answers. Despite the learner's fake screams and pleas to stop, 65% of participants obeyed an authority figure's commands to administer the maximum shock.

The study revealed how authority can override personal morals, explaining behaviors like conformity and obedience in harmful situations. Milgram's work highlights the dangers of blind obedience and has influenced our understanding of group behavior, ethical decision-making, and historical events involving authority-driven harm. These findings underscored the ease with which ordinary people can be led to act against their better judgment, highlighting the potency of psychological manipulation.

In modern society, dark psychology finds its applications across various fields, often in ways that are both subtle and pervasive. In marketing, for instance, companies use sophisticated persuasion techniques to influence consumer behavior. Advertisers craft messages that appeal to emotions, prompting desires and needs that might not naturally exist. Political propaganda, too, is a fertile ground for dark psychological tactics, where spin and manipulation shape public opinion and sway elections. Politicians and spin doctors employ rhetoric and imagery designed to resonate with the subconscious, tugging at fears and aspirations to manipulate voting behavior. Even in personal relationships, dark psychology can manifest as one partner subtly eroding the other's self-esteem to gain control, a tactic as damaging as it is insidious.

The practice of dark psychology raises significant ethical questions, challenging our moral compass. The debate centers on whether using such techniques is justifiable, even for ostensibly positive ends. When does persuasion cross the line into manipulation? And what is the ethical responsibility of those who understand and wield these powerful tools? Case studies of ethical breaches abound, from corporations exploiting consumer vulnerabilities to governments manipulating citizens through propaganda. Each instance forces us to confront the moral implications of using knowledge of the human mind to influence behavior, often blurring the line between influence and coercion .

This exploration of dark psychology is not just an academic exercise but a practical necessity in our interconnected world. Understanding these tactics equips us to recognize and resist manipulation in personal interactions, media consumption, or political discourse. By shining a light on these dark practices, we empower ourselves to control our decisions and protect our autonomy. Through this understanding, we can build stronger, more respectful relationships and create a society that values transparency and ethical behavior.

## 1.3 Historical Contexts and Cultural Significance

Witchcraft and psychology share a complex and intertwined history that has shaped cultural narratives for centuries. In Europe and America, witch trials stand as grim reminders of humanity's struggle with fear of the unknown. From the 15th to the 18th centuries, thousands of women, and some men, were accused of witchcraft, tortured, and executed. These events were often fueled by societal upheaval, religious fervor, and the need to find scapegoats during difficult times. The Salem witch trials of 1692, a particularly infamous episode, serve as a cautionary tale about the dangers of mass hysteria and the societal consequences of unchecked power. These trials highlighted the destructive potential of fear when it morphs into paranoia, leading communities to turn against their own . These historical events left an indelible mark on cultural perceptions, embedding the image of the witch deep into the collective consciousness as both a figure of fear and a symbol of resistance.

Concurrently, the birth of modern psychology marked a shift in understanding human behavior through scientific exploration. In the late 19th and early 20th centuries, figures like Sigmund Freud and Carl Jung revolutionized how we perceive the mind. Freud's theories on the unconscious, dreams, and personality laid the groundwork for analyzing human behavior through a psychological lens. His ideas challenged long-held beliefs and provided a framework for understanding the complexities of human desires and fears. The emergence of psychology as a discipline offered new insights into the motivations behind actions, influencing societal norms and individual self-perception.

* * *

The cultural impact of witchcraft extends beyond the trials and into ancient civilizations' everyday lives and beliefs. In societies such as in Ancient Egypt and Greece, witchcraft was woven into everyday life. It was a respected practice, often associated with healing and protection, used to commune with the divine and harness natural energies. The practitioners, men and women, held positions of reverence and were believed to have a special connection to the spiritual world. Literature and media have continued to shape the narrative, depicting witches as everything from malevolent hags to wise, mystical figures. This evolution reflects society's changing attitudes towards power, gender, and the unknown, offering new interpretations and reclaiming narratives that were once used to oppress.

The interplay between psychological theories and cultural perceptions of witchcraft is a fascinating study in contrasts and synergies. Carl Jung's work on archetypes and symbolism, for instance, draws parallels between modern psychology and ancient beliefs. Jung explored the idea of the collective unconscious, a shared pool of symbols and themes that appear across cultures and times. Witches, in Jungian terms, can be seen as archetypes representing the shadow self or the untamed spirit, embodying both wisdom and chaos. Psychological analyses of historical witch hunts reveal insights into human behavior, illustrating how fear can be manipulated to control and subjugate. This exploration of witchcraft through a psychological lens provides a deeper understanding of why these narratives persist and how they continue to influence modern culture.

***

Today, the significance of both witchcraft and psychology is evident in their enduring presence in contemporary culture. Witchcraft has seen a resurgence, particularly among younger generations seeking alternative spiritual paths. It offers a way to reconnect with nature and the self, providing rituals and practices that foster mindfulness and personal empowerment. Modern media embraces witches as complex characters, reflecting society's ongoing fascination with the mystical and the unknown. Meanwhile, psychology continues to evolve, offering tools to navigate the complexities of modern life. Its principles are applied in various fields, from mental health to marketing, shaping the way we understand ourselves and interact with the world.

The enduring relevance of these fields lies in their ability to adapt and resonate with contemporary needs. As society becomes more aware of the subtle forces that shape human behavior, the insights offered by witchcraft and psychology become invaluable. They provide frameworks for understanding the world and ourselves, empowering individuals to protect themselves from manipulation and embrace their own power. This chapter serves as a reminder that the past informs the present, and by understanding these historical contexts, we can better navigate the challenges of today's world, armed with knowledge and insight.

***

## 1.4 Common Misconceptions and Ethical Considerations

Misunderstandings about witchcraft and dark psychology abound, often clouded by myths and misconceptions that have persisted through the ages. Many people imagine witchcraft as a practice filled with sinister rituals and malevolent intent, largely due to folklore and media portrayals. However, these depictions are far from accurate. White witchcraft, in particular, focuses on healing and protection, yet it often gets lumped together with darker practices like black magic. This misunderstanding not only misrepresents the true nature of white witchcraft but also discredits the positive impact it can have on individuals and communities. Similarly, dark psychology is frequently misunderstood as a nefarious toolkit wielded by those with malicious intent. In reality, understanding psychological manipulation can foster awareness and provide insights into human behavior, helping us recognize when we are being manipulated. Yet, the myths persist, painting a picture of manipulation as an act of evil rather than a complex psychological interaction that can occur in everyday life.

Ethics form the foundation of both witchcraft and psychology. In white witchcraft, the principle of "harm none" emphasizes the ethical responsibility to avoid causing harm through magical practices. It also upholds respect for free will, requiring spells and rituals to be performed only with informed consent. These principles promote compassion and respect, reflecting the core values of white witchcraft.

Similarly, psychology relies on strict ethical standards to protect individuals and ensure accountability. Informed consent is vital, requiring psychologists to secure explicit permission before therapy or research. This safeguards participants' autonomy and ensures they fully understand their involvement. Confidentiality further reinforces trust and protects personal information, preserving the field's integrity. These ethical guidelines uphold human dignity while advancing knowledge responsibly.

Balancing belief in witchcraft with scientific skepticism requires an open but critical approach. Rational examination of practices—magical or psychological—leads to deeper understanding and appreciation. By integrating belief with critical thinking, we explore new ideas while avoiding blind faith or unproven claims.

In today's fast-paced world, combating misinformation is important. Addressing myths about witchcraft and maintaining psychological ethics fosters respect and informed decision-making. This balanced approach enhances understanding, prevents harm, and promotes meaningful engagement with the world.

## 1.5 Tools of the Trade: Witchcraft and Psychology

In the domain of white witchcraft, the tools used are as symbolic as they are functional, serving as conduits for the energies practitioners seek to channel. The athame, a ritual knife, is not for physical cutting but for directing energy and casting protective circles. It represents the element of air or fire, depending on tradition, and is often used to mark sacred space. The chalice, another essential tool, symbolizes water and femininity, holding the essence of the divine within its cup. It is used in rituals to represent unity and the flow of life. The wand, often crafted from wood, channels energy and represents the element of air or fire as well. Unlike the athame, the wand is a gentler tool, directing energy with a softer touch. Herbs and crystals also play a significant role, each possessing unique properties that enhance spells and rituals. Lavender, for instance, is known for its calming effects, while quartz can amplify energy and intentions. These natural elements connect the practitioner to the earth, grounding their magic in the physical world.

In contrast, dark psychology employs an entirely different set of tools and techniques, focusing on understanding and influencing behavior. Behavioral analysis is at the forefront, allowing practitioners to decode the patterns and motivations that drive human actions. These include personality assessments and observational techniques that reveal underlying traits and tendencies. Techniques for persuasion and influence are also critical, drawing from principles of social psychology to sway decisions and actions subtly. Methods such as the foot-in-the-door technique, where small requests pave the way for larger ones, demonstrate the nuanced art of influence. These tools, used ethically, can enhance understanding and communication, though they carry the potential for manipulation when wielded with less noble intentions.

***

In today's digitalized world, both witchcraft and psychology have adapted their traditional tools to fit modern contexts. Digital tools have become a staple for many practitioners of white witchcraft, offering new ways to engage with ancient practices. Smartphone apps can track lunar phases, suggest rituals, and even serve as digital grimoires where spells and notes are stored. These innovations make the practice more accessible, allowing ordinary people to integrate magic into their daily lives seamlessly. Similarly, in psychology, apps and software have revolutionized the field, providing platforms for behavioral assessments, stress management, and even therapy. These tools democratize access to psychological insights, empowering individuals to take control of their mental health.

The intersection of witchcraft and psychology presents intriguing opportunities for interdisciplinary approaches, blending the mystical with the scientific. Meditation, a practice common to both fields, serves as a bridge, enhancing focus and mindfulness. Coupled with mental exercises from psychology, such as visualization and cognitive restructuring, it offers a powerful method for personal transformation. Moreover, psychological principles can inform the design of rituals, making them more effective and personally meaningful. Understanding the psychological impact of symbols and metaphors can deepen the ritual experience, allowing practitioners to engage more fully with their intentions. This fusion of disciplines enriches both fields, fostering innovation and new ways of understanding the self and the world.

As we investigate the complexities of modern life, these tools—whether rooted in ancient tradition or cutting-edge technology—offer guidance and support. They empower individuals to tap into their inner wisdom, harness their strengths, and protect themselves from external influences. By embracing the tools of both witchcraft and psychology, we open ourselves to a wealth of possibilities, each tool a key to unlocking potential and understanding. This exploration of tools and techniques highlights the diverse ways we can engage with and shape our experiences, blending the seen and unseen, the mystical and the practical.

## 1.6 Bridging the Gap: Integrating Old and New Knowledge

In our rapidly changing world, the wisdom of ancient traditions and the insights of modern psychology can harmonize to create a powerful means of self-protection. Ancient spells, once whispered in secret, can be translated into modern language, making them accessible and relevant to today's challenges. This adaptation allows us to preserve the essence of these rituals while aligning them with contemporary understanding. By integrating psychological insights into traditional practices, we can deepen their effectiveness. Imagine a simple spell for protection that incorporates mindfulness and visualization techniques. The spell becomes not just a ritual but a holistic practice that engages both mind and spirit. This synthesis allows for a more profound connection to the intention behind the magic, empowering you to protect yourself with greater awareness and clarity.

Innovation thrives at the intersection of these two disciplines. By blending elements of witchcraft with psychological practices, we open the door to creative ways of enhancing personal empowerment. Hybrid rituals, for instance, can incorporate mindfulness techniques, grounding individuals in the present moment as they perform their magical workings. This combination fosters a deeper sense of control and focus, essential for effective self-protection. Affirmations, long a staple of psychological practice, can be woven into spell work, amplifying the intent with the power of positive thinking. These affirmations act as a verbal talisman, reinforcing the desired outcome and fortifying the practitioner's resolve. This creative fusion invites exploration and experimentation, encouraging practitioners to craft unique rituals that resonate with their personal needs and goals.

The practical applications of this integrated knowledge are vast, offering tangible benefits in daily life. Personalized protection plans can be crafted using a blend of spells and psychological strategies, tailored to the specific challenges and threats one faces. These plans might include daily rituals for maintaining energy boundaries, combined with cognitive exercises to strengthen mental resilience. In conflict resolution, psychological insights can illuminate the underlying dynamics at play, while magical practices provide tools for calming emotions and creating a space for constructive dialogue. This dual approach empowers individuals to navigate life's challenges with confidence and clarity, drawing on the strengths of both traditions.

As we look to the future, the possibilities for integrating ancient and modern knowledge are endless. This is a dynamic field ripe for continued research and experimentation. Practitioners are encouraged to cultivate a spirit of curiosity and innovation, continuously developing new practices that harness the best of both worlds. Fostering a community of learners can facilitate this growth, providing a supportive network for sharing insights and experiences. Such a community can serve as a catalyst for collective advancement, where ideas are exchanged, and new practices are born from collaboration and shared discovery

In embracing this integration, we find ourselves on a path of empowerment and protection that is both timeless and timely. The wisdom of the past, coupled with the insights of the present, provides a robust framework for navigating the complexities of modern life. This approach not only equips us with tools for personal security but also enriches our understanding of ourselves and the world around us. As we continue to explore and expand upon these practices, we unlock new potentials, forging a path forward that is both enlightened and empowering. The journey of blending ancient wisdom with modern insight is one of discovery and transformation, offering a tapestry of knowledge that is as rich and varied as the traditions themselves.

# Recognizing Manipulation and Protective Rituals

Please picture this: You're in a crowded room, laughter and chatter filling the air, yet you feel inexplicably drained. There's no logical reason for it—you've had a good night's sleep, you're well-fed, and you're surrounded by people you know. And yet, you feel as if the very essence of your energy is being siphoned away. You might be in the presence of an energy vampire, a person who, intentionally or not, feeds off the emotional vitality of others. These individuals can leave you feeling exhausted, overwhelmed, and emotionally depleted, often without you even realizing it.

## 2.1 Energy Vampires

Energy vampires are more common than you might think and can lurk in any social setting—from your workplace to your circle of friends, or even within your family. They are characterized by certain traits and behaviors that drain those around them. One of the key hallmarks of an energy vampire is their constant need for attention, always steering conversations back to themselves and demanding emotional investment from others. They often engage in manipulative or guilt-inducing tactics, playing the victim to elicit sympathy and support. Chronic negativity is another common trait, as they frequently wallow in drama and seek to involve others in their emotional turmoil. This behavior can be draining, leaving you feeling like you're carrying their burdens along with your own.

To identify these energy vampires in your life, it's important to pay attention to how you feel after interacting with certain people. Do you leave conversations feeling uplifted or depleted? Do certain individuals make you feel guilty or obligated to help them? Reflecting on these interactions can provide valuable insights into who might be draining your energy. Consider keeping a journal to track these encounters. Write down how you feel before and after spending time with specific people. Over time, patterns may emerge, revealing those who consistently leave you feeling exhausted or overwhelmed. This self-reflection is an important step in recognizing energy vampires and taking steps to protect yourself from their draining influence.

\*\*\*

Setting clear boundaries is essential for maintaining your emotional and mental well-being when dealing with energy vampires. Assertive communication is key in establishing these boundaries. Clearly express your limits and expectations, and don't be afraid to say no when necessary. It's important to communicate these boundaries calmly and confidently, without guilt or apology. Creating personal space is another effective strategy. This might mean limiting the time you spend with certain individuals or choosing to engage with them only in specific settings where you feel more comfortable. Protecting your energy is not about shutting people out but rather about ensuring that your interactions are healthy and mutually beneficial.

> Reflection Section: Identifying Energy Drainers
>
> Use the following prompts to help identify relationships that may be draining your energy:
>
> - Who do you feel exhausted around, even after brief interactions?
>
> - Which conversations leave you feeling guilty or obligated?
>
> - Are there people who always seem to turn discussions back to their problems, ignoring yours?
>
> Reflect on these questions in your journal to gain clarity on who might be affecting your emotional health.

Take proactive steps to address and mitigate the impact of energy vampires! It is important for maintaining your overall health and well-being. Prolonged exposure to their draining behaviors can lead to stress-related health issues, affecting both your mental and physical states. Recognize the signs and set boundaries, reclaim control over your energy and protect yourself from unnecessary emotional strain. This empowerment allows you to engage more meaningfully with the world around you, ensuring that your interactions are positive and enriching

## 2.2 Rituals for Aura Cleansing and Protection

Your personal energy, please imagine it as a luminous gas surrounding you, a vibrant aura that reflects your physical, emotional, and spiritual well-being. This aura, however, is not impervious. Daily interactions, stress, and negative influences can cloud it, leading to feelings of fatigue and confusion. Recognizing when your aura is cluttered is vital. You might feel persistently tired, irritable, or overwhelmed, even when there's no apparent reason. Regular aura cleansing helps restore balance, inviting clarity and positivity back into your life. It is an act of self-care, maintaining your energetic health much like you would your physical body. Just as you clean your skin, cleansing your aura removes the emotional and spiritual grime accumulated throughout the day, allowing your true essence to shine through.

To cleanse your aura, find a quiet space and stand or sit comfortably. Close your eyes and take deep breaths, visualizing a bright, white light surrounding you. Imagine this light dissolving negativity and filling you with positive energy. You can use a smudging tool like sage or palo santo, waving the smoke gently around your body, or hold a cleansing crystal such as selenite or clear quartz. As you do, repeat a simple affirmation, like, *"I release negativity and welcome peace and balance."* Finish by grounding yourself—place your feet firmly on the ground and visualize roots connecting you to the Earth. Start with this easy method and adjust the affirmation to resonate with yourself as time goes on and you get more used to these practices.

The act is both symbolic and practical, creating a palpable shift in the atmosphere.

Today these traditional practices have evolved to fit modern lifestyles, offering new ways to achieve the same cleansing effects. Guided visualizations have become a popular method for aura cleansing, allowing you to cleanse your energy field through the power of your mind. By visualizing a bright light enveloping your body, you can mentally sweep away any lingering negativity, restoring your aura's natural vibrancy. Sound therapy, too, offers a modern twist on an ancient practice. Instruments like singing bowls or tuning forks create vibrations that resonate with your energy field, helping to clear and balance your aura. The sound waves penetrate deep into your being, releasing tension and promoting harmony. These techniques are easily integrated into daily routines, offering quick yet effective ways to maintain your energetic health.

Creating your own personalized aura cleansing ritual is a deeply empowering process tailored to resonate with your unique needs and preferences. Start by choosing elements that speak to you personally. Perhaps you feel drawn to the soothing scent of lavender or the calming effect of a particular crystal. Incorporate these elements into your ritual, allowing them to enhance your cleansing process.

Affirmations are a powerful tool to include. Repeating positive statements during your ritual reinforces your intention to cleanse and protect your energy. These affirmations serve as a verbal shield, fortifying your aura against negativity. The beauty of a personalized ritual lies in its flexibility and adaptability, allowing you to experiment and discover what truly works for you.

> Personal Reflection: Craft Your Own Ritual for Aura Cleansing
> - Consider what resonates with you. Do you prefer the scent of sage, the sound of a singing bowl, or the feeling of saltwater on your skin?
>
> - Think about affirmations that align with your goals. What positive statements would reinforce your energy and intent?
>
> Write down your choices and combine them into a ritual that feels right for you.

Incorporating these practices into your life not only cleanses your aura but also nurtures your overall well-being. Regularly engaging in aura cleansing rituals creates a sanctuary of calm and clarity within yourself, protecting your energy and enhancing your connection to the world around you. As you embrace these practices, you build a foundation of strength and resilience, empowering you to navigate life's challenges with grace and confidence.

## 2.3 Psychological Defense Mechanisms

Each day, our minds navigate a complex web of thoughts and emotions. To protect against distress, we often rely on psychological defense mechanisms without even realizing it. These mental strategies help shield us from anxiety and internal conflict, making it easier to function in social situations.

A common example is **denial**, where we refuse to accept reality to avoid uncomfortable truths. Another is **projection,** where we attribute our own undesirable feelings or thoughts to someone else, deflecting self-awareness and responsibility. **Rationalization**, a more subtle mechanism, involves reshaping facts to make an event or impulse feel less threatening, masking its true emotional impact with logic.

While these mechanisms can provide short-term relief, relying on them too heavily can create long-term challenges. Recognizing these patterns is the first step toward healthier emotional processing and a more authentic way of living.

Building mental resilience is key to protecting yourself from manipulation, which can often be subtle and insidious. Cognitive-behavioral strategies provide effective tools for this, helping you reframe negative thoughts and challenge unhelpful beliefs. Actively questioning assumptions and exploring alternative perspectives strengthens your mental defenses against manipulative tactics.

Mindfulness practices are equally important for emotional regulation. By staying present in the moment, you develop the ability to observe your thoughts and feelings without judgment. This awareness helps you respond thoughtfully instead of reacting impulsively. Regular mindfulness exercises, such as focused breathing or body scans, deepen your connection to your internal state. Over time, this fosters calm and clarity, even in challenging situations.

Manipulation tactics, such as gaslighting and love bombing, are designed to destabilize and control. **Gaslighting** involves making someone doubt their reality, causing them to question their perceptions and memories. Over time, this can erode confidence and create dependence on the manipulator's version of events. **Love bombing**, on the other hand, uses excessive affection and attention to gain control early in a relationship. While seemingly positive, it often masks a deeper intent to manipulate.

Recognizing these tactics is paramount to maintaining your autonomy. By understanding the signs, you can protect yourself from doubting your experiences and emotions. Awareness is your first line of defense, helping you trust your intuition and preserve your sense of self.

Practicing emotional detachment is another valuable skill in handling manipulation. Detachment doesn't mean apathy—it's the ability to observe your emotions without being consumed by them. Visualization exercises can support this. Imagine a protective barrier around you, allowing you to witness events without absorbing negativity. This mental practice creates a buffer between your emotions and external influences, safeguarding your well-being.

By regularly practicing such techniques, you build resilience, stay centered, and make decisions with clarity rather than emotional turmoil. This sense of stability empowers you to navigate manipulative behaviors with confidence.

## 2.4 The Language of Manipulation: Spotting Red Flags

*Manipulation* often cloaks itself in language that seems benign on the surface but carries a heavy undercurrent of control. The language of manipulation weaves guilt into its fabric, making you feel responsible for someone else's emotions or actions. Phrases like "If you really cared, you would..." or "After all I've done for you..." aim to bend your will by exploiting your sense of duty and compassion. This guilt-inducing language is a hallmark of manipulative behavior, designed to twist your emotions until you comply with the manipulator's desires.

*Passive-aggressive communication* is another common strategy. It manifests in veiled criticisms or backhanded compliments, where the true intent is hidden beneath a facade of politeness. Statements such as "It's fine, I didn't expect you to understand anyway" or "You're always so busy, I don't want to bother you" carry a sting that lingers, making you question your actions and intentions. Despite their subtlety, these words can be deeply unsettling, leaving you with a sense of unease and self-doubt.

Manipulation often hides behind inconsistency, creating a fog of confusion that clouds your perception. When actions contradict words, it signals a disconnect that can undermine trust and clarity. Someone might promise support but consistently fail to show up in meaningful ways, leaving you questioning their reliability. This inconsistency serves as a tool to destabilize your sense of reality, making it easier for the manipulator to sway your thoughts and decisions. Additionally, manipulative individuals frequently shift blame, deftly avoiding responsibility for their actions. They might say, "If you hadn't done that, I wouldn't have reacted this way," subtly placing the onus on you for their behavior. This blame-shifting erodes accountability, allowing the manipulator to maintain control while you grapple with self-blame.

It is important to cultivate critical listening skills for discerning manipulation early on. Active listening exercises can sharpen your ability to detect subtle cues and intentions in conversations. Practice being fully present during interactions, focusing on both the words spoken and the tone used. Notice discrepancies between what is said and how it is said, paying close attention to body language and facial expressions. Being attuned to these nuances can reveal underlying motives that might otherwise go unnoticed. Familiarizing yourself with red flag phrases, such as those that evoke guilt or shift blame, equips you with a mental checklist to assess the true nature of the conversation. Recognizing these patterns allows you to remain grounded and centered, resisting the pull of manipulation.

When facing manipulative language, responding effectively requires a blend of assertiveness and clarity. Assertive communication techniques empower you to express your thoughts and feelings without aggression or submission. Use "I" statements to articulate your perspective, such as

"I feel uncomfortable when..." or "I need clarity on...". This approach centers your emotions and needs, reducing the likelihood of escalating conflict. Setting clear expectations is equally vital, establishing boundaries that define acceptable behavior. Clearly communicate your limits, and be prepared to enforce them if necessary. By stating your expectations calmly and confidently, you assert your right to a respectful and transparent interaction, protecting yourself from manipulation.

Ultimately, recognizing and responding to manipulative language is a skill that strengthens your ability to navigate relationships with confidence and integrity. By understanding the nuances of manipulative communication, you protect yourself from its insidious effects, ensuring that your interactions are grounded in honesty and mutual respect. This awareness fosters healthier connections, where open dialogue and genuine understanding take precedence over hidden agendas and emotional coercion.

## 2.5 Sigils for Psychological Resilience

Creating sigils for psychological resilience combines creativity with purpose, turning intentions into powerful symbols. Sigils are unique designs crafted to embody specific goals or affirmations. Traditionally used in magical practices, they can also serve as modern tools for mental strength and protection against negativity. In this context, sigils act as visual anchors, reinforcing resilience and fortifying your emotional defenses.

To create a sigil, start with a clear intention or affirmation, such as "I am protected" or "I am resilient." Write it down, then remove the vowels and repeating consonants, leaving a condensed string of letters. Arrange these letters into a simple, personal design that resonates with you. This process transforms your intention into a visual form, embedding your focus and energy into the sigil. The result should feel meaningful and empowering—a symbol of your inner strength.

Once your sigil is designed, the next step is to activate and charge it. This involves infusing it with energy and purpose. Meditation works well for this, helping you channel your focus into the symbol. As you meditate, imagine the sigil glowing with light, pulsing with your intention. You can also use elements like fire or water for activation. Hold the sigil over a candle flame to energize it or immerse it in water to charge it with resilience. These elements amplify your intention and seal it within the design.

***

To keep the sigil's influence present in your life, incorporate it into your surroundings or daily routine. Place it in areas where you spend time, like your desk or bedroom, to create a supportive environment. You can also embed it into wearable items like jewelry or clothing, keeping its energy close to you. This constant presence serves as a subtle reminder of your resilience, boosting confidence and mental strength throughout your day.

***

Personalizing sigil use is vital for maximizing their effectiveness. Select symbols and designs that resonate with you personally, as these will carry the most significant impact. The process of choosing and designing a sigil is deeply personal, reflecting your unique journey and the qualities you wish to cultivate. By imbuing your sigils with personal meaning and intention, you create powerful tools that align with your individual path, providing tailored protection and resilience against the challenges you face.

***

## 2.6 Developing Intuition to Detect Deceit

Intuition is often described as a gut feeling or an inner voice that offers subtle guidance. It's a natural skill we all have, though many of us don't actively develop it. Strengthening your intuition can be a powerful way to detect deceit and navigate complex social dynamics.

Mindfulness meditation is an effective way to cultivate intuition. By focusing on the present moment and observing your thoughts without judgment, you quiet the mind and create space for insights to emerge. Regular meditation enhances your ability to sense subtle changes in energy and intention, sharpening your awareness of deception.

Journaling dreams and insights is another useful technique. Dreams tap into the subconscious, often revealing hidden truths and emotions. Keeping a dream journal helps you identify recurring patterns and symbols that connect with your intuition, offering guidance in daily life.

Recognizing intuitive signals is key to trusting your inner voice. Intuition often manifests as physical sensations, like a flutter in the stomach or tingling on the skin. These signals can act as early warnings of dishonesty or danger. Pay attention to how your body reacts in different situations and note any patterns that arise when you sense something is off. With practice, you'll become more attuned to these signals and rely on them with confidence.

Intuition is a personal experience that varies from person to person. Take time to explore and understand how it works for you. Techniques like daily intuition journaling can help. Reflect on your experiences and note any gut feelings or impressions you've had. This practice strengthens your connection to your inner voice.

Visualization exercises can also boost intuitive clarity. Picture a moment when your intuition guided you well. Focus on the feelings and sensations from that experience to reinforce your trust in this ability. Repeating these exercises builds confidence, making it easier to apply intuition in real-life situations.

***

Using intuition in daily life can lead to better decisions and deeper understanding of others' intentions. When faced with choices, quiet your mind and tune into how each option feels intuitively. This inner guidance often reveals insights that logic alone might miss, helping you make more authentic and aligned decisions.

Many successful people credit their achievements to moments when they trusted their instincts, even against external advice. These stories highlight the power of intuition to guide us toward truth and authenticity, serving as a reliable compass in human interactions.

# Practical Applications of Witchcraft and Psychology

Please imagine you're standing barefoot on a lush, green lawn, feeling the cool earth beneath your feet. As you breathe deeply, you become aware of a sensation of peace flowing through you. This is grounding—an essential technique for maintaining emotional and mental stability, especially in times of stress. Grounding connects you to the earth, anchoring you in the present moment and providing a stable foundation from which to face life's challenges. It helps regulate emotions, offering a calming counterbalance to the chaos of modern life. When grounded, you feel more centered, focused, and capable of handling whatever comes your way.

## 3.1 Grounding

Traditional grounding methods, often rooted in witchcraft, offer accessible ways to incorporate this practice into your daily routine. Earthing, for example, is a simple yet powerful technique that involves direct physical contact with the earth. Walking barefoot on grass, sand, or soil allows your body to absorb the earth's natural energy. This connection not only grounds you but also has been shown to reduce stress and promote a sense of well-being. Visualization exercises can enhance this process, engaging your mind and spirit in the act of grounding. Imagine roots extending from the soles of your feet deep into the earth, anchoring you securely. This visualization reinforces your connection to the earth, providing a mental anchor that you can return to whenever you feel unsteady.

Psychological approaches to grounding complement these traditional methods, offering additional tools for emotional regulation. Deep breathing exercises are a cornerstone of psychological grounding techniques, helping to calm the nervous system and bring your focus back to the present. Concentrating on your breath can slow your heart rate and reduce anxiety. Inhale deeply through your nose, allowing your belly to expand, then exhale slowly through your mouth. This simple act of mindful breathing can be done anywhere, providing an instant sense of calm. Progressive muscle relaxation is another effective technique involving the systematic tensing and relaxing of muscle groups throughout the body. This practice reduces physical tension and promotes a sense of relaxation, making it easier to maintain emotional stability in stressful situations.

Creating a personalized grounding routine that integrates both witchcraft and psychological elements can enhance your overall well-being. Consider incorporating grounding rituals into your morning or evening routine, setting the tone for the day or unwinding before sleep. Begin your ritual by selecting grounding stones or crystals known for their stabilizing properties, such as hematite or black tourmaline. Carry these stones with you or place them in your environment to harness their grounding energy. As you hold or touch these stones, focus on their weight and texture, allowing them to draw away excess energy and center your mind. This tactile connection reinforces your grounding practice, creating a tangible link to the earth's stabilizing force.

---

Interactive Element: Personal Grounding Routine Checklist

- Choose your grounding stones or crystals.
- Plan a daily time for grounding exercises.
- Combine earthing with breath work or visualization.
- Reflect on the effects in a journal.

---

Incorporate these elements into a personalized routine that resonates with you, adapting the practices to fit your lifestyle and preferences. Whether through traditional or psychological methods, grounding offers a pathway to greater emotional and mental stability, empowering you to face life's challenges with resilience and poise. Embrace the grounding process as a daily practice, and experience the profound impact it can have on your sense of well-being and personal empowerment.

## 3.2 Ritualistic Practices for Inner Strength

Inner strength is not just a notion; it's the quiet force that carries you through life's challenges. In the context of witchcraft and psychology, inner strength embodies resilience, self-awareness, and emotional fortitude. It's the ability to remain steady and confident despite the chaos around you. This strength is rooted in a profound understanding of oneself, recognizing both limitations and potential. It involves the courage to face fears and the confidence to pursue aspirations. In essence, it's about possessing the mental and emotional resources to handle adversity with grace. Cultivating inner strength is akin to building a sturdy foundation that supports personal growth and well-being.

*Empowerment rituals* play a significant role in enhancing inner strength, providing both symbolic and practical support. Candle rituals are a powerful method, channeling the transformative energy of fire. To perform such a ritual, choose a candle that resonates with your intention—perhaps red for courage or yellow for confidence. As you light it, focus on the flame, envisioning your inner strength growing with its light. Let the candle burn as you meditate on your personal power, reaffirming your resilience. *Affirmation circles* offer another form of ritual, where you gather with like-minded individuals to share and reinforce positive beliefs. Together, you can create a sacred space for empowerment, each person contributing affirmations that build collective strength.

\*\*\*

*Psychological exercises* complement these rituals, reinforcing resilience and fortitude through introspection and self-compassion. Engaging in self-compassion exercises allows you to treat yourself with the same kindness you extend to others. This involves recognizing your struggles without judgment and offering yourself understanding and support. Visualization techniques can further enhance your sense of personal power. Picture yourself as a strong, unyielding tree, deeply rooted in the ground yet flexible enough to sway with the wind. This imagery strengthens your mental resolve, reminding you of your capacity to endure and thrive.

\*\*\*

Combining rituals with psychological practices creates a holistic approach to inner strength, amplifying their effects. After performing a candle ritual, consider journaling your thoughts and feelings. Reflect on the insights revealed during the ritual, capturing them in words. This practice deepens your connection to the experience, allowing you to explore and solidify your newfound strength. Group empowerment activities also blend these elements, providing both communal support and individual growth. Gather with others to share your experiences, engage in collective rituals, and discuss psychological strategies for empowerment. These activities foster a sense of belonging and shared purpose, reinforcing the strength you cultivate within yourself.

## 3.3 Mindfulness in Witchcraft: Staying Present

Mindfulness, a powerful tool in both witchcraft and psychology, invites you to stay present in the moment, fostering focus and clarity. It's about being fully engaged with your surroundings and inner experiences without judgment. This practice can significantly enhance your ability to respond to life's stressors with calmness and intentionality. In witchcraft, mindfulness elevates your rituals, helping you connect deeply with your intentions and the energies you wish to harness. By cultivating this presence, you increase your capacity for insight and intuition, grounding your actions in awareness and purpose.

Incorporating mindfulness into your witchcraft practices enriches your rituals and daily life. Consider mindful spell casting, where you focus intently on each element of your spell, from the words you speak to the objects you use. This conscious engagement ensures that your energy is aligned with your intentions, amplifying the spell's effectiveness. Meditation with crystals can also deepen your practice, as each crystal's unique energy can guide your focus and intention. Hold a crystal in your hands, close your eyes, and breathe deeply, allowing its energy to flow through you. This process not only enhances your connection to the natural world but also strengthens your inner clarity and resolve.

Psychological techniques for mindfulness complement these practices, offering practical ways to cultivate presence and awareness. Mindful breathing exercises are simple yet profound, focusing your attention on each breath as it enters and leaves your body. This practice calms the mind and reduces stress, creating a space for reflection and insight. Sensory awareness activities further enhance mindfulness, engaging your senses fully in the present moment. Pay attention to the textures, sounds, and scents around you, noticing details you might typically overlook. This heightened awareness can lead to greater appreciation and understanding of your environment and yourself.

Incorporating mindfulness into your daily routine can transform ordinary moments into opportunities for presence and peace. Mindful eating, for instance, involves savoring each bite of food, noticing its flavors and textures. This practice enhances your enjoyment of meals and promotes healthier eating habits by encouraging you to slow down and listen to your body's signals. Mindful walking is another accessible activity, where each step becomes a meditation, connecting you to the earth beneath your feet. As you walk, focus on the rhythm of your steps and the sensations in your body, allowing your mind to settle into a state of calm awareness.

Journaling offers yet another avenue for mindfulness, providing a space to capture your thoughts and feelings. Set aside time each day to write freely, without concern for grammar or structure. This process allows you to explore your inner landscape, uncovering patterns and insights that might otherwise remain hidden. By engaging in these daily practices, you cultivate a deeper connection to the present moment, enhancing your ability to navigate life's challenges with clarity and grace. As you integrate mindfulness into your life, you may find a renewed sense of empowerment and peace, grounded in the awareness of each passing moment.

## 3.4 Protective Spells for Everyday Situations

In everyday life, protective spells serve as a shield, guarding against the unseen forces that can disrupt our peace. If you have reservations about the word 'spell,' think of it as a strong intention. I will be using the word spell for easy writing purposes. These spells are crafted with intention, forming an energetic barrier that wards off negativity and harm. They act as silent sentinels, safeguarding your well-being as you navigate the complexities of modern existence. The purpose behind protective spells is to empower you, ensuring that you remain centered and secure, no matter the challenges you encounter. There are various types of protective spells, each tailored to different needs and situations. Some focus on personal protection, forming a bubble of safety around your aura, while others extend their reach to protect your home, your loved ones, or even your travels. These spells are not just about defense; they are proactive measures that help you maintain balance and harmony in your life.

Simple yet effective spells can be woven into your daily routine with minimal materials, making them accessible to anyone seeking protection. One such spell is the protection jar spell, which involves creating a small container filled with protective herbs, crystals, and symbols. To craft this spell, select a jar and fill it with items like salt, rosemary, and amethyst—each chosen for its protective properties. As you place each element into the jar, focus on your intention for protection, infusing it with your energy. Seal the jar and place it in a safe space within your home, allowing it to act as a beacon of safety and security. Reflective warding spells offer another layer of defense, designed to bounce negative energy back to its source. For this spell, visualize a mirror surrounding your aura, reflecting any harm or ill will away from you. This mental image serves as a powerful deterrent, keeping negativity at bay.

Incorporating personal symbols into your spell casting adds a layer of personalization, enhancing the spell's effectiveness. Personal items can serve as talismans, infused with your unique energy and intention. Consider using a piece of jewelry, a favorite stone, or a written affirmation as part of your spell. These items hold significance for you, making them potent tools in your protective arsenal. When casting a spell, hold your chosen item and focus on its meaning, drawing on its power to fortify your defenses. The connection between you and your talisman strengthens the spell, aligning it with your personal energy and intent. This practice enhances the spell's power and deepens your connection to the ritual, making it a more meaningful and transformative experience.

Adapting spells to specific everyday scenarios ensures that your protective measures are as effective as possible. For travel safety, consider a spell that focuses on smooth and secure journeys. Before embarking on a trip, visualize a protective bubble around your vehicle, keeping you safe from harm. You might also carry a small charm or crystal in your luggage, serving as a talisman for protection on the road.

In the workplace, protective spells can help shield you from negative influences and maintain a positive environment. A simple desk ritual might involve placing a small plant or crystal on your desk and infusing it with intentions of peace and productivity. As you go about your workday, let this object serve as a reminder of your protective spell, reinforcing your mental and emotional barriers.

Protective spells are not just about shielding yourself from harm; they are about creating a space where you feel empowered and in control. They allow you to take an active role in your well-being, using the tools of witchcraft to shape your environment and experiences. These spells offer a sense of agency, reminding you that you have the power to protect and nurture yourself in a world full of uncertainties. By integrating protective spells into your daily life, you cultivate a sense of security and peace, empowering yourself to face whatever comes your way with courage and confidence.

## 3.5 Psychological Strategies for Boundary Setting

Boundaries are an integral part of maintaining mental health and ensuring personal safety. They act as invisible lines that define where your emotional and psychological space begins and ends, protecting you from unwanted intrusion or influence. Establishing these boundaries allows you to maintain a sense of self, ensuring that your needs and feelings are respected in your interactions with others. Without clear boundaries, you may be overwhelmed by others' demands, leading to stress and resentment. Emotional boundaries help safeguard your feelings, ensuring that you do not take on the emotional burdens of others. Psychological boundaries, on the other hand, protect your thoughts and beliefs, allowing you to maintain your own identity without undue influence. These boundaries create a safe space where you can thrive, nurturing your mental well-being and reinforcing your personal integrity.

Effective boundary setting often begins with assertive communication techniques. These techniques involve expressing your needs and limits clearly and respectfully, without aggression or apology. Start by using "I" statements, such as "I need time to myself to recharge" or "I feel uncomfortable when my space is invaded." This approach centers your experience, fostering understanding without placing blame. Additionally, identifying your personal limits is imperative. Reflect on what feels comfortable and what doesn't, taking note of situations that make you feel uneasy or drained. Recognize these moments as indicators of where boundaries are needed. By understanding and articulating your limits, you empower yourself to maintain control over your interactions, creating an environment that respects and honors your needs.

Incorporating rituals into your boundary-setting practices can reinforce these psychological limits, enhancing their strength and resilience. Consider rituals that involve visualization, where you imagine a protective barrier surrounding you. This mental image acts as a shield, reminding you of your boundaries and reinforcing your resolve to uphold them. You might also create a physical representation of your boundaries, such as drawing a circle around yourself with salt or placing a protective stone at the entrance to your home. These tangible symbols serve as constant reminders of the boundaries you've set, imbuing them with power and intention. Rituals fortify your boundaries and provide a moment of reflection and recommitment to your personal well-being.

Despite your best efforts, boundary pushers—those who challenge or disregard your limits—are inevitable. Handling these situations requires both patience and persistence. When confronted by someone who tests your boundaries, remain firm but polite. Reiterate your limits clearly, and if necessary, distance yourself from the situation to maintain your integrity. It's also important to engage in self-reflection regarding the effectiveness of your boundaries. Regularly assess their impact on your mental and emotional health, making adjustments as needed. Consider journaling about situations where your boundaries were tested, reflecting on what worked and what didn't. This practice encourages continuous growth, helping you refine your strategies and maintain a healthy relationship balance.

## *3.6* Integrating Shadow Work for Self-Awareness

Shadow work is a profound psychological practice that delves into the parts of ourselves we often hide or deny. This concept, introduced by Carl Jung, refers to the "shadow" as the unconscious facets of our personality that we have chosen to ignore or suppress. These can include traits we deem undesirable, such as anger or jealousy, but also positive attributes we are reluctant to acknowledge. Engaging with the shadow is critical for personal growth, as it allows us to confront these hidden aspects, bringing them into the light where they can be understood and integrated. By accepting these neglected parts, you can achieve a more complete and authentic self, fostering greater self-awareness and emotional resilience.

To embark on this path of self-discovery, several techniques can guide you in exploring and integrating your shadow self. One effective method is journaling, which encourages introspection and self-reflection. Begin with prompts that challenge you to explore your dislikes and desires, such as "What traits in others irritate me?" or "What qualities do I envy?" These questions can reveal projections of your shadow, illuminating areas of personal growth. As you write, allow your thoughts to flow freely, without judgment, acknowledging whatever arises. Guided meditations can also facilitate shadow exploration, offering a safe space to encounter and engage with these aspects. Through visualization, you can form a dialogue with your shadow, asking questions and seeking understanding. This practice helps to dissolve the barriers between your conscious mind and the hidden depths of your psyche, paving the way for healing and transformation.

Witchcraft rituals provide a unique opportunity to integrate shadow aspects, combining symbolism with intention to facilitate this process. Shadow release ceremonies, for instance, offer a powerful way to acknowledge and let go of these hidden parts. In such a ritual, you might write down the aspects of your shadow you wish to release on a piece of paper, then safely burn it as a symbolic act of transformation. As the paper turns to ash, visualize the release of these traits, making space for acceptance and growth. This ritual not only allows for the symbolic release of unwanted traits but also reinforces your commitment to embracing your whole self. The act of ritualizing this process adds a layer of intention and mindfulness, deepening your connection to the work and its transformative potential.

The integration of psychological insights with ritual practices can enhance the effectiveness of shadow work, creating a synergy that supports more profound healing. Incorporating therapy techniques, such as cognitive restructuring, into your rituals can help you challenge and reframe negative thought patterns associated with your shadow. This approach encourages you to view these traits with compassion and understanding, transforming them from sources of shame into opportunities for growth. Visualization exercises can further support this integration, offering a way to embody acceptance and unity. Picture yourself embracing your shadow, welcoming it as a valuable part of who you are. This visualization fosters a sense of wholeness, allowing you to integrate these aspects into your conscious identity with love and acceptance.

***

By engaging in shadow work, you embark on a self-discovery path leading to greater personal insight and empowerment. This practice invites you to face the parts of yourself you have long ignored, transforming them into allies on your journey to wholeness. Through a combination of psychological techniques and witchcraft rituals, you can embrace your shadow with compassion, unlocking the door to deeper self-awareness and personal growth. This integration enriches your understanding of yourself and strengthens your resilience, equipping you to navigate the complexities of life with confidence and authenticity. As you continue this exploration, you will find that embracing your shadow is not a one-time event but an ongoing process of acceptance and transformation, offering new insights and opportunities for growth at every turn.

We explored grounding, inner strength, mindfulness, protective spells, boundaries, and shadow work. These tools and practices provide a solid framework for enhancing personal power and protection. As we move forward, we'll explore emotional healing and recovery, exploring how ancient and modern techniques can support your journey toward holistic well-being.

# Emotional Healing and Recovery

I sit quietly on my porch, a single candle flickering. I watch the flame dance, its glow casting shadows. The sun had just begun to set, casting a gentle orange hue across the sky. I feel blessed. I have a small, worn journal filled with memories of a past I am ready to release. When I open the pages, I Take a deep breath and begin to write, pouring out the words. With each word, a weight lifts, carried away by the warm breeze. This ritual is a sanctuary, a moment of healing and release, and it is here that I find strength and peace.

## 4.1 Healing Rituals

Healing rituals like this offer a powerful avenue for addressing past trauma. These rituals serve as sacred spaces where you can confront and release the emotional burdens that weigh you down. They provide structure and intention, guiding you through the process of healing with compassion and purpose. By engaging in these rituals, you create a bridge between your past and present, allowing for transformation and renewal. This connection between ritual and emotional healing taps into the deep well of wisdom within you, encouraging reflection and growth. Rituals are not merely acts; they are journeys into the heart, where you can find solace and understanding.

There are various healing rituals to explore, each offering unique pathways to recovery. Candle lighting ceremonies are a gentle yet profound way to release pain and invite light into your life symbolically. As you light a candle, imagine its flame consuming the darkness within, illuminating your path forward. Please focus on the warmth and light, allowing it to fill you with hope and clarity.

Water cleansing rituals also hold transformative power. Water, a symbol of purification and renewal, washes away the residues of trauma, leaving you refreshed and revitalized. Engage in a ritual bath, adding herbs or oils to enhance the experience. As you submerge yourself, visualize the water absorbing your pain and carrying it away. Both rituals invite you to be present, to honor your journey, and to embrace the healing process with openness.

Establishing a secure and meaningful space for these rituals is essential for promoting a healing atmosphere. Choose a tranquil environment where you feel secure and at peace. This might be a quiet corner in your home, a secluded spot in nature, or any place that brings you comfort. Use protective symbols and items to fortify this space, such as crystals, sacred objects, or symbols of protection. These elements ground your practice, creating a boundary between you and the outside world. This sacred space becomes a refuge, a place where you can explore your emotions without fear or judgment.

Incorporating personal elements into your rituals enhances their healing power, making them uniquely yours. Personal artifacts or mementos hold memories and emotions, serving as tangible reminders of your journey. Include these items in your rituals, allowing their presence to guide and support you. Integrate personal affirmations to further strengthens the ritual, reinforcing your intention and commitment to healing. Speak these affirmations aloud or write them down, infusing them with belief and determination. This personalization transforms the ritual from a generic practice into a deeply meaningful experience, aligning it with your personal path and needs.

> Interactive Element: Craft Your Healing Ritual
> - Identify a candle or water-based ritual that resonates with you.
>
> - Choose a location that feels safe and peaceful.
>
> - Gather personal items or mementos that hold significance.
>
> - Write affirmations that support your healing journey.

By engaging in these healing rituals, you honor yourself and your journey. You create a space where past trauma can be acknowledged and released, allowing for growth and renewal. These practices empower you to take an active role in your healing, guiding you toward a future filled with hope and possibility.

## 4.2 Psychology of Emotional Recovery

Emotional recovery is a multi-faceted process, deeply embedded in psychological principles that guide healing. At its heart, emotional recovery involves emotional processing and regulation, two crucial components that enable you to navigate the aftermath of trauma. Emotional processing allows you to confront and make sense of your experiences, transforming chaos into coherence. It involves engaging with your emotions, understanding their origins, and integrating them into your narrative. This is where emotional regulation comes into play, providing strategies to manage the intensity of your feelings. By learning to regulate emotions, you create a space for healing, where you can respond to distress with calm and clarity rather than reactionary overwhelm. The brain's remarkable ability to adapt, known as neuroplasticity, underpins this process. Due to its neuroplasticity, your brain can form new connections and pathways, facilitating recovery by reshaping how you process and respond to emotional stimuli. This adaptability is the brain's phenomenal ability for growth and change even after deep-seated trauma.

\*\*\*

Understanding the stages of emotional recovery can serve as a roadmap, guiding you through the often difficult phases of healing. Initially, acknowledgment and acceptance are the center of healing. Acknowledgment involves recognizing the reality of your trauma and its impact on your life. Acceptance, on the other hand, means embracing your emotions without judgment, allowing yourself to feel without resistance. This stage lays the groundwork for deeper healing, as it opens the door to processing and integration. Processing involves consciously engaging with your emotions, exploring their root causes and meanings. It's about allowing to go into the depths of your experience, seeking understanding and insight. Integration follows, where you incorporate the lessons learned from your trauma into your daily life. This stage is about absorbing your experiences into your inner being, allowing them to inform and enrich your journey forward. These stages are not linear; they ebb and flow, reflecting the dynamic nature of healing.

\*\*\*

To facilitate emotional recovery, several psychological techniques can be invaluable. **Cognitive restructuring** exercises are one such tool, helping you reframe negative thoughts and beliefs. By challenging cognitive distortions, you can shift your perspective, fostering a more balanced and positive outlook. This technique empowers you to break free from limiting beliefs, opening the door to new possibilities. **Emotional Freedom Techniques (EFT)**, or tapping, offer another avenue for healing. This method involves tapping on specific acupressure points while focusing on emotional distress. The rhythmic tapping helps release emotional blockages, promoting relaxation and reducing stress. EFT can be a powerful tool for self-soothing, allowing you to regain control over your emotional landscape. These techniques, when practiced consistently, build resilience and foster emotional well-being, equipping you to face life's challenges with greater confidence and grace.

A support system plays an indispensable role in the emotional recovery process, providing a network of individuals who offer understanding and encouragement. Building connections with supportive people can create a safety net, offering a space where you can express your feelings without fear of judgment. Whether it's friends, family, or support groups, these connections nurture your healing journey, reminding you that you are not alone. Accessing professional counseling services can further enhance your recovery, offering expert guidance and tailored interventions. Therapists provide a safe and structured environment for exploring your emotions, helping you navigate the complexities of trauma with compassion and skill. They can offer insights and techniques that deepen your understanding and support your progress, serving as allies in your healing. By building a diverse support system, you create a rich network of care and connection, bolstering your resilience and enriching your path to recovery.

## 4.3 Cleansing Rituals for Emotional Renewal

Cleansing rituals hold a special place in the realm of emotional renewal, offering a pathway to release negative emotions and energies that cling to the spirit like a stubborn fog. These rituals serve as a form of emotional detox, shedding the layers of stress and anxiety accumulated from daily life. When engaging in cleansing rituals, you create an opportunity to reset your emotional state, inviting a sense of peace and rejuvenation. The act of cleansing is not merely a physical gesture but a symbolic release, a declaration that you are ready to let go of what no longer serves you. This process allows you to reclaim your emotional vitality, paving the way for new beginnings and personal growth. As you cleanse, you make space for positive energies to flow freely, nurturing your well-being and fortifying your resilience against life's challenges.

Traditional cleansing practices have long been used to facilitate emotional renewal, drawing on the natural elements to purify and protect. Smudging with sage or sweetgrass is a time-honored technique that harnesses the purifying power of smoke to clear away negative energies. As the fragrant smoke curls through the air, it carries away emotional toxins, leaving behind a sense of clarity and calm. This ritual can be performed in your living space or around your body, creating a protective barrier that shields you from negativity. Ritual baths offer another avenue for cleansing, combining the soothing properties of water with the healing essence of herbs and oils. By immersing yourself in a bath infused with lavender, chamomile, or rose petals, you invite a deep relaxation that penetrates both body and spirit. The water absorbs emotional burdens, leaving you feeling refreshed and revitalized. These practices are powerful reminders of the interconnectedness between nature and healing, drawing on the earth's resources to restore balance and harmony.

***

Incorporating modern adaptations into cleansing rituals allows for a personalized approach to emotional renewal, making these practices accessible and relevant to contemporary life. Aromatherapy diffusers offer a convenient and effective way to integrate the benefits of essential oils into your environment. You create a tranquil atmosphere that supports emotional release and relaxation by dispersing calming scents such as lavender or eucalyptus. The gentle aroma envelops you, encouraging deep, restorative breaths that calm the nervous system. Sound healing with tuning forks introduces another layer of renewal, using vibrations to harmonize your energy field. These vibrations penetrate deeply, dissolving emotional blockages and restoring equilibrium. Integrating these modern adaptations enhances the cleansing process, tailoring it to fit your unique needs and lifestyle.

Designing a personalized cleansing ritual invites you to engage with these practices on a deeper level, aligning them with your emotional goals and preferences. Begin by selecting herbs and oils that resonate with your intentions for cleansing. Consider what qualities you wish to invoke—perhaps clarity, peace, or strength—and choose ingredients that embody these attributes. Incorporating meditation and visualization further enriches the ritual, allowing you to focus your mind and amplify your intention. As you cleanse, visualize negative energies dissolving, replaced by a radiant light that fills you with warmth and vitality. This mental imagery enhances the effectiveness of the ritual, creating a holistic experience that nurtures both mind and spirit. By crafting a ritual that reflects your personal journey, you transform the act of cleansing into a meaningful and empowering practice.

## 4.4 Self-Affirmation in Magic and Mind

Self-affirmation is a cornerstone in magical practices and psychological well-being alike, anchoring you in positive beliefs and self-worth. In the realm of magic, affirmations serve as verbal spells, crafting a reality grounded in intention and possibility. When you affirm your strengths and potential, you lay a foundation for the magic you wish to weave into your life. Psychologically, self-affirmations reinforce your self-concept, buffering against the negative self-talk that can undermine your confidence. These positive statements act as mental armor, offering protection against doubt and fear. By consistently affirming your worth and capabilities, you cultivate a resilient mindset supporting personal growth and emotional stability. This dual role of self-affirmation underscores its power to transform how you perceive yourself and engage with the world.

Creating powerful affirmations is an art that begins with clarity and intention. To craft effective affirmations, use the present tense to frame each statement as if it is already true. This technique aligns your subconscious with the reality you seek to manifest, bridging the gap between desire and existence. Positive language is necessary, steering clear of negatives or limitations. Rather than saying, "I am not afraid," choose "I am courageous and confident." This subtle shift directs your focus toward what you wish to embody rather than what you wish to avoid. Incorporating personal goals and values into your affirmations further enhances their power. Consider what you truly desire—be it love, success, or peace—and ensure that your affirmations reflect these aspirations. By aligning your affirmations with your core values, you create statements that resonate deeply, amplifying their impact on your psyche and spirit.

Integrating affirmations into magical rituals enhances their potency, weaving intention into the fabric of your practice. Chanting affirmations during rituals infuses the air with your desires, creating a harmonic resonance that aligns with the energies you seek to harness. As you chant, visualize your affirmations taking shape, enveloping you in a cocoon of possibility and protection. Writing affirmations on spell components—such as candles, herbs, or charms—further embeds your intention into the physical realm. Each time you light a candle or hold a charm, you activate the magic of your affirmation, reinforcing its presence in your life. This seamless integration of affirmations into rituals transforms them from mere words into powerful catalysts for change, bridging the gap between intention and action.

Incorporating affirmations into your daily routine is a practical way to keep your intentions at the forefront of your mind. Affirmation journaling provides a structured space to explore and solidify your affirmations, inviting you to reflect on their meaning and impact. Set aside time each day to write your affirmations, allowing the process of putting pen to paper to deepen your connection to your words. Morning and evening affirmation routines bookend your day with intention, setting a positive tone for the hours ahead and offering closure at night. As you wake, speak your affirmations aloud, letting their energy infuse your morning with possibility and purpose. Before sleep, repeat them softly, allowing their echoes to weave into your dreams. These practices create a rhythm of affirmation, embedding your intentions into the very fabric of your day.

***

## 4.5 The Role of Forgiveness in Healing

Forgiveness, at its core, is the conscious choice to release feelings of resentment or vengeance toward those who have harmed you, regardless of whether they truly deserve your forgiveness. It's important to distinguish forgiveness from condoning behavior. When you forgive, you are not excusing or justifying the actions that caused pain. Instead, you are opting to free **yourself** from the emotional shackles that bind you to that hurt. This release opens the door to healing, allowing you to move forward without the burden of past grievances weighing you down. It's a profound act of self-liberation, granting you the peace to reclaim your emotional landscape and redefine your narrative.

Embracing forgiveness can bring a cascade of psychological benefits, contributing significantly to emotional healing. By choosing to forgive, you lighten the emotional burdens that often manifest as anger, bitterness, or a desire for retribution. These feelings, if left unchecked, can seep into every facet of your life, clouding your judgment and impacting your relationships. Forgiveness alleviates this weight, creating space for positivity and growth. Additionally, it plays a pivotal role in improving mental health and overall well-being. Studies indicate that people who practice forgiveness experience reduced stress, lower levels of anxiety and depression, and a more optimistic outlook on life. This emotional clarity fosters resilience, equipping you to face future challenges with renewed strength and perspective.

Rituals can serve as a powerful catalyst in the process of forgiveness, offering structured methods to facilitate emotional release. One such ritual involves the act of burning letters of release. This symbolic gesture allows you to articulate your feelings on paper, expressing the hurt and betrayal in a tangible form. Once written, these letters are set aflame, signifying the transformation of pain into ashes. As the paper burns, visualize the release of your resentment, watching it dissipate with the smoke into the ether. Water release ceremonies provide an alternative method, using the cleansing properties of water to wash away emotional residue. As you immerse an item or symbol of your grievance in water, imagine it dissolving, carried away by the currents. This ritual fosters a sense of renewal, leaving you with a clean slate.

Practical steps can further support your journey toward forgiveness, grounding the emotional release in actionable exercises. Guided visualizations offer a pathway to release resentment, inviting you to envision each hurt as a tangible object that you can gently let go. Please picture yourself standing on the edge of a flowing river, holding these objects in your hands. As you release them into the water, feel the relief of letting go, their weight lifted from your shoulders. Developing empathy and understanding is another crucial aspect of forgiveness. This involves stepping into the shoes of those who have wronged you, seeking to understand their motivations and struggles. By building empathy, you soften the edges of your anger, opening the door to compassion. This practice does not excuse their actions but allows you to recognize the humanity within us all, paving the way for genuine forgiveness.

***

## 4.6 Building Resilience Through Ritual

Resilience is the ability to bounce back from adversity, to adapt and thrive despite challenges. It's like a rubber band that stretches but doesn't break. For long-term emotional health, resilience is crucial. It equips you to handle stress, recover from setbacks, and remain focused on your goals. Resilient individuals tend to have a positive outlook, strong coping mechanisms, and an ability to learn from difficult experiences. They embrace change and view it as an opportunity for growth. This mindset fortifies against life's inevitable hardships and enhances overall well-being. When cultivating resilience, you build a foundation that supports you through life's ups and downs, empowering you to face challenges with courage and confidence.

Rituals can play a profound role in strengthening resilience, offering structured practices that ground and inspire. **Stone-carrying rituals** are a simple yet powerful way to cultivate resilience. By carrying a stone that symbolizes strength and stability, you create a tangible connection to the earth's grounding energy. Throughout the day, touch the stone and visualize its solidity transferring to you, reinforcing your inner strength. Rituals of gratitude and appreciation also enhance resilience by shifting focus from what is lacking to what is abundant. Begin or end your day by listing things you are grateful for, acknowledging the positives in your life. This practice nurtures a mindset of appreciation, providing a buffer against negative thoughts and fostering emotional resilience.

In addition to rituals, psychological practices offer valuable tools for building resilience. **Positive visualizations and mental rehearsals** can transform your approach to challenges. Imagine yourself in a difficult situation, then visualize a successful outcome. This mental practice prepares your mind for real-life scenarios, boosting confidence and problem-solving skills. Journaling for reflection and growth further supports resilience by providing a space to process experiences and emotions. Regular journaling allows you to track progress, identify patterns, and reflect on lessons learned. This introspection fosters self-awareness and adaptability, key components of resilience.

Integrating ritual and psychology creates a holistic approach to resilience, combining the strengths of both disciplines. By blending rituals with cognitive-behavioral exercises, you can enhance their effectiveness. For example, after a ritual of gratitude, engage in a cognitive exercise where you challenge negative thoughts and replace them with positive affirmations. This integration reinforces the ritual's impact, embedding gratitude and positivity into your mindset. Developing a resilience-building routine ensures these practices become a regular part of your life. Create a schedule that incorporates both rituals and psychological exercises tailored to your unique needs. This routine acts as a personal resilience plan, equipping you with a toolkit to navigate life's challenges with strength and grace.

As we wrap up this chapter, please reflect on how resilience and emotional healing come together to build strength and growth. These practices set the stage for what's next, where the journey of empowerment continues with fresh insights and tools to enhance your life.

# Ethical Considerations and Responsible Practice

This chapter invites you to explore the two paths, into the light or veering into the darker realms, examining the ethical considerations of using magic and the responsibility that comes with wielding such power.

## 5.1 The Ethics of Hexing and Curses

Hexing and curses are among the most controversial aspects of magical practice, often misunderstood and shrouded in fear. At their core, hexes are spells intended to bring misfortune or bad luck to another, often seen as minor acts of harm. Curses, by contrast, carry a heavier weight, designed to cause significant and long-lasting harm. These practices have been part of many magical traditions throughout history, serving as tools for justice or deterrents against wrongdoing. In the past, hexes and curses were sometimes used to exact retribution or protect communities from perceived threats. However, the ethical implications of such practices remain a topic of heated debate among witches and practitioners today.

The moral implications of using hexes and curses extend beyond the immediate effects on the target, touching upon deeper questions of intent and consequence. At the heart of this discussion lies the concept of karma and the threefold law, which suggests that the energy you put into the world will return to you threefold. This principle acts as a cautionary tale for those considering harmful magic, warning of potential repercussions that may rebound upon the caster. Engaging in hexing or cursing can also have psychological effects on the practitioner, fostering negative emotions such as anger and resentment. These emotions can create a cycle of negativity, impacting the practitioner's mental and emotional well-being. The decision to cast a hex or curse requires careful reflection on one's intentions and the potential consequences, both seen and unseen.

***

For anyone seeking alternatives to harmful magic, ethical witchcraft practices offer a variety of options that align with the principles of protection and justice without causing direct harm. Binding spells, for instance, are designed to prevent an individual from causing harm, effectively neutralizing negative intentions. These spells focus on containment rather than aggression, offering a protective barrier that shields the practitioner and others from potential threats. Reflective spells provide another alternative, sending negative energy back to its source without adding to the cycle of harm. These spells act as mirrors, deflecting harmful intentions while maintaining the practitioner's ethical integrity.

***

Reflecting on historical examples of curses and their outcomes can offer valuable insights into the potential consequences of these practices. One famous case is the so-called "mummy's curse," associated with the opening of Tutankhamen's tomb in the 1920s. Despite the myth that those involved faced mysterious deaths, studies found no significant difference in survival rates between those exposed and unexposed to the curse, suggesting that the curse's power was more fiction than fact. This case highlights how curses, while powerful in lore, may not hold the tangible effects often attributed to them. Such reflections serve as reminders of the importance of questioning and critically evaluating the narratives surrounding hexes and curses, encouraging practitioners to consider the ethical dimensions of their magical practices.

> Reflection Section: Evaluating Intentions
> - Consider a situation where you felt wronged. Reflect on your initial reaction and the emotions it stirred.
>
> - Ask yourself: What are my true intentions in responding? Are they rooted in protection, justice, or something else?
>
> - Consider the long-term consequences of acting on these intentions. How might they affect you and others involved?

By embracing ethical alternatives and reflecting on historical examples, you can navigate the complexities of magical practice with wisdom and integrity, ensuring that your actions align with your values and contribute to a more positive and balanced world.

## 5.2 Responsible Use of Dark Psychology Insights

Dark psychology, with its nuanced understanding of human behavior and influence, offers powerful insights into the mind. Yet, wielding such knowledge requires a careful ethical approach. The application of dark psychology should never bypass informed consent. This concept, fundamental in both psychological practice and daily interactions, ensures that individuals are fully aware of and agree to the influence being exerted over them. Informed consent respects the autonomy and dignity of others, allowing them to make decisions based on clear, honest information. Without it, the line between ethical influence and manipulation blurs, leading to potential exploitation. As someone who understands the potent capabilities of dark psychology, you have a responsibility to avoid using these insights for manipulation or coercion. Your intent should always align with respecting others' autonomy, fostering trust and transparency in your interactions.

Recognizing personal and ethical boundaries is critical when considering the application of psychological techniques. Establishing clear intent before engaging in any form of influence is essential. This means being fully aware of your motivations and ensuring they align with ethical standards. Are you aiming to empower and uplift, or are you veering towards control? Respecting individual autonomy involves acknowledging each person's right to make their own choices, free from undue influence. This respect forms the foundation of ethical practice, promoting honesty and integrity. Boundaries, both personal and professional, act as guides that keep interactions respectful and fair. They help maintain clarity and trust, ensuring that your use of psychological insights supports and uplifts rather than diminishes.

When used ethically, dark psychology insights can be powerful tools for positive influence. They can enhance motivation, bolster confidence, and encourage healthy communication practices. Techniques that boost motivation might include helping someone visualize their goals or reinforcing their sense of accomplishment. These methods can inspire and drive individual people toward personal and professional growth. Promoting healthy communication means creating a space where open dialogue and mutual respect can flourish. By actively listening and engaging with empathy, you help others feel heard and valued. This approach empowers individuals, strengthens relationships, and builds a solid foundation of respect and collaboration.

Avoiding harmful practices is paramount in maintaining ethical standards. Recognizing signs of coercive control is super important, as these behaviors can subtly erode autonomy and well-being. Coercive control often manifests as manipulation or emotional abuse, where one person exerts power over another through intimidation or dependency. Being vigilant about these signs allows you to intervene and prevent potential harm. Deceptive tactics, such as misinformation or emotional manipulation, should be avoided at all costs. These practices betray trust and undermine the ethical use of psychology. Instead, strive for transparency and honesty, ensuring that your actions reflect your integrity and respect for others.

As you navigate the complexity of dark psychology, remember that your intentions and actions have the power to shape outcomes. By adhering to ethical principles and prioritizing informed consent, you create a space where influence becomes a tool for empowerment rather than manipulation. This approach not only protects those you interact with but also enriches your practice, aligning your actions with your values and fostering a culture of respect and growth.

## 5.3 Consent and Boundaries in Magic

In the realm of magic, the principles of informed consent are as vital as the air we breathe. Just as in any interpersonal interaction, seeking permission before casting spells that affect others is a fundamental tenet. Consent is not just a formality; it's a recognition of respect and autonomy. Whether you are crafting a love spell or a protection charm for another, obtaining explicit permission ensures that the recipient is open to the magical influence. Without consent, even the most well-intentioned spell can infringe upon someone's personal sovereignty. This respect extends to communal rituals, where informed consent means that every participant is aware of the ritual's purpose and agrees to be part of it. In these settings, transparency about the intentions and effects of the magic being performed is crucial. This promotes an environment where everyone feels safe and respected, allowing the magic to flow freely and harmoniously among participants.

Establishing boundaries in magical practice is as important as the spells themselves. Clear personal and group boundaries serve as the framework within which magic can be practiced ethically and responsibly. Personal boundaries are your lines in the sand, defining what is acceptable and what is not in your magical interactions. Group boundaries, on the other hand, are collectively agreed upon rules that ensure everyone in a communal setting feels comfortable and respected. Communicating these boundaries effectively requires openness and clarity. It's about stating your limits without ambiguity and listening to others with empathy and understanding. This dialogue is not a one-time conversation but an ongoing process that evolves with the needs and experiences of those involved. Maintaining clear and open lines of communication and you create a foundation of trust and mutual respect, essential for any magical endeavor.

***

Navigating complex situations where consent and boundaries might be challenged can be like walking a tightrope. In group settings, boundary violations can occur, often unintentionally, leading to discomfort or conflict. Addressing these issues head-on is imperative. Open discussions should be encouraged, allowing everyone to voice their concerns and feelings without fear of retribution. These conversations can be difficult but are necessary for maintaining harmony and trust within the group. Handling conflicts of interest requires sensitivity and fairness. It's about finding a balance that respects individual boundaries while considering the group's dynamics and objectives. When conflicts arise, mediation and compromise can help find a solution that honors all parties involved. By approaching these situations with patience and an open heart, you can navigate the complexities of consent and boundaries with grace and integrity.

Promoting respectful practice in all magical endeavors starts with adopting ethical guidelines as a framework for action. These guidelines serve as a moral compass, ensuring that your practice aligns with your values and the principles of respect and consent. Encouraging ongoing dialogue about consent is another crucial step. This means regularly revisiting the topic within your magical community, ensuring that everyone remains aware of its importance and feels comfortable discussing it. This dialogue is not about imposing rules but about fostering understanding and cooperation. Respectful practice is about creating a culture where consent is ingrained in every aspect of magic, from the simplest spell to the most complex ritual. It's about nurturing an environment where everyone feels valued and empowered, where magic becomes a collaborative and transformative force for good.

## 5.4 Ethical Dilemmas in Psychological Manipulation

When engaging with psychological manipulation, you may encounter ethical dilemmas that challenge your understanding of influence and autonomy. These dilemmas often arise when trying to balance the desire to influence others with the need to respect their autonomy. Imagine a situation where you possess the skills to influence a colleague's decision for what you genuinely believe is their benefit. Yet, the ethical question remains: are you respecting their right to make independent choices? This grey area in persuasion can be tricky. While your intentions might be positive, the methods you employ could inadvertently undermine their autonomy. It's very important to navigate these ethical waters with care, always questioning whether your influence respects the other person's freedom to choose. Recognizing the fine line between persuasion and manipulation helps maintain trust and integrity in your interactions.

To address ethical dilemmas in psychological practices adopt decision-making frameworks to provide guidance. Two prominent approaches are utilitarianism and deontology. Utilitarianism suggests that the morality of an action is determined by its outcomes, aiming for the greatest good for the greatest number. When applying this to psychological influence, consider whether your actions will result in positive outcomes for all parties involved. Deontology, on the other hand, emphasizes duties and principles over consequences. This approach advocates adhering to ethical guidelines, regardless of the potential outcomes. By applying these frameworks to real-life case scenarios, you can evaluate your actions more objectively. Reflect on whether your methods align with ethical standards and consider the broader impact of your influence. These frameworks serve as valuable tools, helping you navigate the complexities of ethical decision-making with clarity and purpose.

Managing power dynamics when applying psychological insights can be challenging, as imbalances can lead to unintended consequences. Power imbalances often occur in relationships where one person holds more knowledge, authority, or influence than the other. Recognizing these imbalances is the first step toward equitable interactions. For example, in a mentor-mentee relationship, the mentor's role is to guide and support, not to control or dictate. Strategies for equitable interactions include active listening, empathetic communication, and fostering an environment of mutual respect. Encouraging open dialogue allows for the exchange of ideas and perspectives, empowering both parties to contribute meaningfully. By being mindful of power dynamics, you can create a space where everyone feels valued and heard, strengthening the foundation of your relationships.

Reflective practice is a powerful tool for continuously evaluating your ethical behavior, allowing you to grow and learn from your experiences. Journaling ethical concerns and resolutions can provide insight into your thought processes and decision-making patterns. Document your reflections and you gain clarity on your actions, motivations, and the impact on others. This practice encourages self-awareness and accountability, fostering personal and professional development. Seeking feedback from peers and mentors further enhances your reflective practice. Constructive feedback offers alternative perspectives, challenging you to reconsider your assumptions and biases. Engaging with others in this way helps refine your ethical understanding and encourages ongoing growth. Through reflective practice, you build a mindset of continuous improvement, ensuring that your use of psychological manipulation aligns with your values and ethical standards.

## 5.5 Balancing Skepticism with Open-mindedness

In both witchcraft and psychology, balancing skepticism with open-mindedness is a dance of discernment. You are standing at the intersection of ancient wisdom and modern science, where each offers valuable insights, yet demands careful scrutiny. Skepticism serves as a protective shield, encouraging critical thinking and inquiry. It helps you question the validity of claims, ensuring that beliefs and practices are grounded in reality rather than fantasy. This critical lens is super important, especially in fields where misinformation can easily take root. Yet, being too skeptical can lead to cynicism, closing you off from new ideas and possibilities. That's where open-mindedness comes in, inviting you to consider diverse perspectives and embrace innovation. It encourages curiosity and exploration, opening doors to knowledge and growth. Together, skepticism and open-mindedness create a balanced approach, allowing you to navigate both disciplines with wisdom and insight.

Evaluating information critically is an essential skill in both disciplines, as it enables you to assess the credibility of sources and identify logical fallacies and biases. In an age where information is abundant and often conflicting, discerning truth from fiction requires vigilance. Start by examining the source of the information. Is it reputable and well-regarded within the community? Consider the author's credentials and the evidence provided to support their claims. Be wary of logical fallacies, such as circular reasoning or ad hominem attacks, which can undermine an argument's validity. Bias, too, can skew information, so it's essential to recognize when personal or cultural biases may influence perspectives. When applying these techniques, you sharpen your ability to evaluate claims critically, ensuring that your beliefs are informed and balanced.

Encouraging open exploration of ideas while maintaining skepticism is a delicate balance. It involves engaging in respectful debates and discussions, where differing viewpoints are not only tolerated but welcomed. This exchange of ideas enriches your understanding, providing a broader context for your beliefs. Exploring diverse perspectives and practices allows you to expand your horizons, challenging assumptions and fostering innovation. It's through this open exploration that you can discover new insights and refine your understanding. By approaching new ideas with curiosity rather than judgment, you create a fertile ground for growth and transformation.

Developing a personal philosophy that incorporates both skepticism and openness requires reflection and adaptability. Begin by examining your personal beliefs and values. What do you hold dear, and why? Reflect on how these beliefs have shaped your perspective and consider how they might evolve in light of new evidence or experiences. Adapting beliefs based on new information is a hallmark of intellectual humility, acknowledging that knowledge is ever-changing and that growth often requires letting go of outdated ideas. By embracing this adaptability, you cultivate a philosophy that is both resilient and flexible, capable of navigating the complexities of witchcraft and psychology with grace and insight.

## 5.6 Ensuring Harm Reduction in Practices

In both witchcraft and psychology, the principles of harm reduction serve as a vital foundation for safe and responsible practice. At its core, harm reduction is about minimizing risk and potential harm while fostering a culture of safety and care. This approach acknowledges that while certain practices carry inherent risks, these can be mitigated through thoughtful planning and consideration. In witchcraft, this might mean being mindful of the energies invoked and ensuring that spells are cast with clear, positive intentions. In psychology, it involves recognizing the potential impact of interventions and ensuring they are applied ethically and safely. Harm reduction is not about eliminating risk entirely, but rather about taking proactive steps to manage and reduce it, creating an environment where both practitioners and participants feel secure and respected.

Strategies for safe practice are equally important in both magical and psychological contexts. Before embarking on any ritual or intervention, conducting a risk assessment is fundamental. This involves identifying potential risks and considering how they might be mitigated. Ask yourself: What are the possible outcomes, and how can I ensure they align with my intentions? In group settings, implementing safety protocols is vital to ensure everyone's well-being. This might include establishing clear guidelines for participation, ensuring that all voices are heard, and creating a space where individuals feel comfortable expressing concerns. These protocols help to create an atmosphere of trust and mutual respect, where everyone is aware of the boundaries and expectations. By prioritizing safety, you lay the groundwork for a practice that is both ethical and effective.

Creating supportive environments that prioritize harm reduction requires commitment and effort. Training and education on harm reduction principles are invaluable tools for empowering practitioners and participants alike. You can foster a community that is informed and conscientious by providing access to resources and learning opportunities. Encourage open dialogue about harm reduction, allowing individuals to share their experiences and insights. This exchange of knowledge enriches the community and also reinforces a culture of accountability and care. Peer support plays a role in this process, offering individual participants the chance to learn from one another and provide feedback. You create a resilient community that is equipped to handle challenges and navigate complexities with confidence by building networks of support,.

Continuous evaluation and improvement are significant components of responsible practice. Regularly reviewing safety protocols ensures they remain relevant and effective, adapting to new insights and experiences. This ongoing reflection encourages a dynamic approach, where practices evolve in response to changing needs and contexts. Incorporating feedback from participants is a main aspect of this process. Actively seek and value input, this demonstrates a commitment to growth and learning. This feedback loop allows for the refinement of practices, ensuring they remain aligned with ethical standards and community values. Continuous improvement is about embracing change and innovation, recognizing that perfection is not the goal, but rather the pursuit of excellence through thoughtful reflection and adaptation.

Embracing these principles of harm reduction, you not only protect yourself and others but also contribute to a culture of ethical and responsible practice. These strategies ensure that your actions are guided by integrity and respect, fostering environments where individuals can explore and grow safely. By prioritizing safety and care, you create a foundation that supports meaningful and transformative experiences, both within yourself and within the communities you engage with.

## Share Your Thoughts and Make a Difference

Your review could be the spark that helps someone discover a whole new world.

By now you know that your words matter – a lot—they can guide, inspire, and even change someone's perspective.

My aim is to reach as many people as possible to get even more light and positivity into our world.

Would you take a moment to help someone you've never met? It's a small action with a big impact.

Reviews are what most people rely on when deciding whether to give a book a chance. By sharing your thoughts, you're not just supporting this book—you're helping it reach the people who need it most, and I would feel honored that you took the time to connect

So, if the idea of lifting up others speaks to you, welcome aboard! You're now part of a community that believes in spreading positivity, knowledge, and empowerment.

Thank you so much for being here and for sharing your voice.

With gratitude,

Selena Blackwood

# Comprehensive Self-Improvement and Growth

Establishing daily routines is like creating a clear plan, helping you navigate life with structure and clarity. These routines provide stability, supporting your mental and emotional health while fostering habits for growth. By setting daily intentions, you stay aligned with your goals, making it easier to achieve meaningful progress.

## 6.1 Setting Routines

Your morning sets the tone for your day. Begin with a simple meditation to calm your mind and focus on the present. Visualization can enhance this practice—imagine your day unfolding with clarity and purpose. See yourself completing tasks with ease, reaching goals, and maintaining calm throughout.

Gratitude journaling is another powerful tool. Reflect on the positive aspects of your life to cultivate a mindset of abundance. Acknowledging what you're thankful for fosters a positive outlook that influences your interactions and decisions. These practices create a strong foundation of intention and resilience to help you navigate challenges with grace.

*\*\*\**

Evening rituals provide a space for reflection and preparation. Reflective journaling offers insights into your thoughts and experiences. Use prompts like, "What did I learn today?" or "How did I overcome challenges?" to guide your reflections. This practice helps identify growth areas and celebrate achievements, setting the stage for a more intentional tomorrow. By ending your day with reflection, you honor your progress and prepare your mind for new opportunities.

*\*\*\**

Incorporating elements of witchcraft can deepen and empower your routines. Crystals and herbs bring natural energies that support your intentions. Keep amethyst nearby during meditation for peace and focus. Use rosemary or sage in tea or incense to purify your space and mind. Simple protection spells can reinforce boundaries and shield against negativity. A few intentional words are enough to create a powerful effect. By blending these elements into your daily life, you draw on ancient wisdom to enrich your modern practice.

---

Reflection Section: Crafting Your Daily Routine
- **Morning**: What elements resonate with you to start the day positively?
- **Evening**: How can reflective journaling enhance your nightly routine?
- **Witchcraft Elements**: What crystals or herbs will you incorporate?

Write down your preferences and experiment to create a routine that feels right for you.

---

## 6.2 Psychological Exercises for Lifelong Learning

Imagine every challenge as a hidden opportunity waiting to be discovered. This mindset forms the foundation of lifelong learning and personal growth. Cultivating a growth mindset means embracing challenges as stepping stones to greater understanding and capability. Viewing failures as feedback rather than defeat transforms setbacks into lessons. Each experience refines your approach and deepens your knowledge. This perspective builds resilience, helping you face life's complexities with curiosity and determination. By consistently seeking growth in every situation, you create a path for continuous improvement and success.

Cognitive exercises are powerful tools for enhancing mental agility and promoting learning. Activities like puzzles and brain training games challenge your mind, stimulating neural pathways and improving cognitive function. These exercises are both engaging and effective, fostering mental flexibility and problem-solving skills. Memory techniques, such as mnemonics and visualization, also support mental sharpness. Regular practice creates a dynamic mental environment, preparing you to adapt to new challenges. Incorporating these habits into your routine boosts memory, speeds up thinking, and cultivates an adaptable mindset.

***

Emotional intelligence is vital for personal and professional growth. It enhances your ability to navigate social interactions with empathy and understanding. Recognizing and managing your emotions, as well as those of others, fosters meaningful connections. Exercises like active listening improve empathy by helping you tune into others' feelings and perspectives. Focus on understanding rather than formulating a response, allowing you to fully grasp the speaker's message. This practice builds trust and respect, leading to stronger relationships and better communication. Developing emotional intelligence also improves conflict resolution and fosters deeper connections, contributing to success in all areas of life.

Reflect on personal growth, it is key to tracking your progress over time. Keeping a growth journal allows you to document experiences, thoughts, and feelings, providing valuable insights. This practice encourages introspection, helping you identify patterns and set actionable goals. Reviewing and adjusting these goals ensures they stay relevant to your evolving needs. Reflection not only reinforces your commitment to growth but also keeps you motivated and accountable. By regularly assessing your journey, you gain clarity on your strengths, areas for improvement, and the steps needed to achieve a fulfilling and intentional life.

***

## 6.3 Integrating Witchcraft into Modern Life

Adapting traditional witchcraft to modern life may seem challenging, but it's entirely achievable with creativity and flexibility. Traditional rituals, often elaborate and time-consuming, can be simplified without losing their essence. Focus on the core components—intention and symbolism. For instance, a full moon ritual requiring hours of preparation can be condensed into a brief meditation with a candle and a few meaningful words. Technology also supports this adaptation. Apps that track lunar phases or serve as digital grimoires help you seamlessly integrate ancient practices into your routine. By embracing these tools, you can honor tradition while meeting the demands of modern life.

Creating a personal spiritual space at home provides a sanctuary for consistent practice. Designate a small area, like a table or shelf, as your altar or sacred corner. Decorate it with items that hold personal significance—crystals, candles, or meaningful objects. These elements enhance the energy of the space and serve as visual reminders of your intentions. This sacred space becomes a retreat from daily chaos, fostering spiritual growth and inner connection.

Incorporating magic into daily tasks transforms the mundane into meaningful rituals. Infuse intention into simple actions, such as stirring your morning coffee clockwise while focusing on your goals. This small act becomes a mindful ritual. Use sigils to subtly influence your environment—draw one for focus or protection in your planner or notebook. Each time you see it, you reinforce your intentions subconsciously. These practices weave magic into daily life, creating a continuous thread of empowerment.

Balancing modern demands with traditional practices requires flexibility and innovation. Small, intentional moments throughout your day can maintain your connection to witchcraft. Engage in brief rituals during your commute or before bed. Respect tradition while embracing innovation to keep your practice relevant and beneficial. By blending ancient wisdom with modern convenience, you create a harmonious and sustainable spiritual path.

## 6.4 Building a Legacy of Empowerment

Your actions ripple outward, influencing not only your immediate environment but also the broader community and family around you. The legacy you build is not just a reflection of who you are—it's a guiding light for those who come after you. It is shaped by your ambitions, the choices you make, and the relationships you cultivate. Through intentional living, you create a legacy that authentically reflects your essence, illuminating the way for others with the wisdom you've gained and the life you've lived.

Sharing your knowledge and experiences is one of the most powerful ways to inspire and empower others. Mentoring allows you to pass on hard-earned wisdom, guiding others as they navigate their own journeys. This is a mutually enriching experience—just as your mentees grow from your guidance, you also gain fresh perspectives and insights from them. Teaching, whether in formal settings or through everyday interactions, offers opportunities to foster resilience and encourage growth in others. Writing personal stories, memoirs, or guides can further extend your reach, providing a lasting source of inspiration and learning for those who seek guidance.

Each story you share becomes a seed, planted in the minds and hearts of others. These seeds grow into a shared legacy of understanding, resilience, and empowerment. By consciously shaping your actions and sharing your journey, you leave behind more than memories—you create a roadmap for others, guiding them to build their own meaningful lives.

\*\*\*

Creating rituals and practices that are sustainable ensures that your legacy endures beyond your lifetime. Developing rituals that can be passed down through generations imbues them with a timeless quality, connecting your descendants to their roots. These practices may evolve, but their foundational principles remain intact, a testament to your foresight and wisdom. Documenting personal practices ensures that they are preserved for future generations, serving as a guide and inspiration. This documentation can take many forms—a handwritten journal, a digital collection, or even a series of videos—each capturing the essence of your practices and the values they represent. By preserving these practices, you create a living legacy that adapts and grows with each new generation, a bridge between past and future.

Celebrating milestones and achievements is crucial in acknowledging both personal and communal growth. Organizing milestone ceremonies provides an opportunity to recognize significant accomplishments, whether they are personal achievements or collective successes. These ceremonies serve as a pause, a moment to reflect on the journey and the progress made. They offer a chance to gather with loved ones, sharing in the joy of success and the lessons learned along the way. Keeping a record of personal growth and achievements further solidifies this process, creating a tangible reminder of the strides made over time. This record becomes a source of motivation, a testament to your resilience and determination. By celebrating these milestones, you affirm your commitment to growth and empowerment, reinforcing the values that shape your legacy.

## 6.5 The Journey of Self-Discovery

Understanding who you truly are is an ongoing process that requires patience, openness, and courage. It's a dynamic process, including change and transformation, each step bringing new insights and revelations about yourself. Embracing change is a vital part of this journey, as it allows you to recognize and honor the evolution of your identity over time. Every experience, whether joyful or challenging, contributes to shaping your understanding of who you are. Welcome these shifts and you align yourself with the natural ebb and flow of life, enriching your personal growth. This process is not a straight path but a winding road filled with opportunities for exploration and self-awareness. Embrace each twist and turn with curiosity and compassion, knowing that each moment of discovery is a step toward understanding your true self.

To facilitate self-exploration, various tools and practices can guide your path. Personality assessments offer a structured way to uncover traits, preferences, and tendencies that define you. These assessments provide a framework for understanding how you interact with the world and make decisions. They can be a starting point for deeper reflection, helping you identify areas for growth and potential paths for development. Journaling serves as another powerful tool, inviting you to engage in self-reflection and introspection. Through writing, you articulate your thoughts and emotions, creating a dialogue with yourself that uncovers hidden patterns and desires. This practice encourages honesty and vulnerability, allowing you to explore your inner landscape without judgment. Together, these tools create a foundation for introspective exploration, offering guidance and clarity as you navigate the complexities of self-discovery.

Authenticity emerges when you embrace your true self, shedding layers of societal expectations and external pressures. It is about honoring your unique voice and expressing it without fear. This authenticity is not a fixed state but a dynamic expression of your evolving identity. Practices that help uncover your true self include meditation, art, or any activity that allows you to connect with your inner essence. These practices encourage self-expression and creativity, freeing you from the constraints of conformity and expectation. Strategies for overcoming societal pressures involve setting boundaries and cultivating a strong sense of self-worth. By prioritizing your values and needs, you create a space where authenticity can thrive. This process requires courage, as it may involve challenging norms and redefining what it means to be true to yourself. Yet, with each step toward authenticity, you strengthen your connection to your inner truth, fostering a sense of fulfillment and purpose.

Creating a personal roadmap for self-discovery provides direction and focus, guiding you through the intricate process of exploring your identity. Setting personal milestones and goals helps chart your progress, offering tangible markers of growth and achievement. These milestones serve as checkpoints, reminding you of your commitment to self-discovery and encouraging persistence in the face of challenges. Reflecting on past experiences informs your future growth, allowing you to draw lessons from the past and apply them to new situations. This reflection fosters a deeper understanding of your journey, revealing patterns and insights that illuminate your path forward. As you design this roadmap, remain open to the unexpected, allowing room for spontaneity and exploration. Your journey is unique, shaped by your experiences, aspirations, and the ever-evolving understanding of who you are. Embrace this process with patience and curiosity, knowing that each step brings you closer to the heart of your authentic self.

## 6.6 Embracing Change Through Ritual and Reflection

Change is an inevitable part of life, a force that can either propel us forward or leave us feeling unmoored. Yet, when viewed with a positive lens, change becomes a powerful catalyst for growth. It challenges us to step out of our comfort zones, to adapt and evolve. This process of adaptation is not always easy, but it is vital for personal development. Embracing change involves seeing it as an opportunity rather than a threat. It's about recognizing that each shift, each transition, brings with it a chance to learn and grow. This mindset allows us to navigate uncertainty with confidence, transforming potential obstacles into stepping stones toward a more fulfilling life.

***

Rituals can provide a structured way to embrace and navigate significant life changes, offering comfort and guidance during times of transition. Transition ceremonies, for instance, mark the beginning of a new chapter. Whether it's a new job, the end of a relationship, or a move to a new city, these ceremonies help to acknowledge and honor the change. They provide a moment to reflect on what has been and set intentions for what is to come. Similarly, rituals for releasing old patterns can be instrumental in letting go of habits or mindsets that no longer serve us. These rituals might involve writing down what you wish to release and then symbolically burning the paper, watching the smoke carry away the old to make room for the new. Such practices can be deeply cathartic, creating a sense of closure and readiness for the next phase of life.

Reflection acts as a powerful tool in adapting to change, offering insights and understanding that can ease the transition. Reflective journaling practices encourage you to explore your thoughts and feelings about the changes you are experiencing. When putting pen to paper, you externalize your internal dialogue, making sense of the chaos and finding clarity amidst uncertainty. This practice helps to identify patterns and lessons, revealing how past experiences can inform future decisions. Meditation on change and impermanence further deepens this reflection. By sitting in stillness, focusing on the breath, and contemplating the transient nature of life, you cultivate a sense of acceptance and calm.

This mindfulness practice allows you to embrace the ebb and flow of life, adapting to change with grace and equanimity.

Using the experience of change to foster resilience is an empowering approach that builds strength and adaptability. By viewing challenges as opportunities for growth, you develop the ability to face adversity with courage and determination. Each experience becomes a lesson in resilience, teaching you how to bend without breaking. Celebrating adaptability and growth is essential in reinforcing this strength. Acknowledge the progress you have made, the hurdles you have overcome, and the skills you have acquired along the way. This celebration need not be grand; it can be as simple as a moment of gratitude or a quiet reflection on how far you have come. By recognizing your growth, you reinforce your resilience, preparing yourself for the changes yet to come. Through this process, you build a foundation of strength and adaptability, ready to face whatever life may bring. As you embrace change, you find empowerment in your ability to adapt and grow, becoming a more resilient and capable version of yourself.

# Advanced Techniques and Personal Empowerment

Have you ever noticed how certain symbols catch your eye, almost speaking to you on a subconscious level? Perhaps it's a design etched into a stone you pass by or a pattern in the clouds that seems to form an image you just can't ignore. These symbols often hold power beyond their simple shapes, connecting with the deeper parts of our mind and spirit. Sigils, crafted with intention, harness this power, becoming potent tools of protection and empowerment. They are not just artistic expressions but vessels of energy, carrying your intentions into the world around you.

## 7.1 Sigils

Sigil crafting is an art steeped in complexity, where layered symbolism and intricate patterns blend to form a powerful talisman. At its core, a sigil is a visual representation of a desire or intention, distilled into a unique symbol. Advanced sigil design involves the incorporation of multiple symbols, each carrying its own meaning, converging into a single, cohesive form. This layering adds depth and strength, creating a multifaceted emblem that resonates on various levels. Sacred geometry, with its timeless patterns and structures, plays a fundamental role in this process. Shapes like the vesica piscis or the flower of life can be woven into your sigil, lending their ancient power to your personal design. These geometric patterns are not only aesthetically pleasing but also carry a vibrational frequency that enhances the sigil's potency, connecting it to universal energies.

Once your sigil is crafted, the next step is to charge and activate it, infusing it with energy and intention. This process can be likened to lighting a fuse, setting the symbol's power into motion. Ritualized activation ceremonies provide a structured approach to this task. By dedicating time and space to the activation, you create an environment that focuses your energy and intent. Incorporate elemental forces—earth, air, fire, and water—to amplify the charging process. Each element brings a unique aspect to the ritual: earth grounds the energy, air circulates it, fire ignites it, and water purifies and sustains it. For example, you might place your sigil on the ground, allowing earth's stabilizing energy to flow through it, or pass it through the smoke of burning herbs to cleanse and energize it. Such rituals not only energize the sigil but also deepen your connection to it, making it a living extension of your will.

Sigils are not static; their power can be sustained and even enhanced through long-term use. Periodic recharging rituals are essential to maintain their effectiveness, much like tending to a garden to ensure it continues to thrive. These rituals can be simple yet profound, involving meditation, visualization, or even re-drawing the sigil to renew its energy. Consider incorporating your sigil into permanent structures, such as etching it onto a favorite piece of jewelry or carving it into a wooden altar piece. This permanence allows the sigil's energy to become a constant presence in your life, subtly influencing and protecting you in your daily activities.

Personalizing your sigil practices ensures they align with your beliefs and goals, making them uniquely yours. Integrate personal totems or symbols into the design to reflect your individual journey and aspirations. These could be animal symbols that resonate with your spirit or abstract shapes that hold personal significance. By embedding these elements, you create a sigil that is not only a tool of protection but also a mirror of your innermost self. This personalization strengthens the bond between you and your sigil, enhancing its effectiveness and ensuring it serves your highest good.

## 7.2 Harnessing the Power of Intentions

Imagine standing before a blank canvas, brush in hand, ready to paint the life you envision. This canvas is your future, and the brush is your intention. Setting clear intentions is like outlining the masterpiece you wish to create. It begins with clarity, the ability to distill your deepest desires into a precise and focused aim. To do this, take a moment to quiet your mind and reflect on what truly matters to you. Align your intentions with your personal values, ensuring they resonate with your core beliefs and aspirations. This alignment acts as a compass, guiding your actions and decisions toward fulfillment. Intention-setting is not just wishful thinking; it's a deliberate act of directing your energy toward specific goals, empowering you to shape your reality.

Rituals can serve as powerful amplifiers of intentions, channeling energy and focus to manifest your desires. Creating intention boards is one such ritual, where you gather images, words, and symbols that represent your goals and arrange them on a board. This visual collage serves as a daily reminder of your aspirations, reinforcing your commitment to them. Another ritual involves the use of affirmations, positive statements that declare your intentions as if they have already been realized. Speak these affirmations aloud, allowing the words to resonate within you. The repetition of affirmations strengthens their impact, embedding them into your subconscious mind, and aligning your thoughts and actions with the outcomes you seek.

Incorporating intention-based practices into your daily routine ensures that your goals remain at the forefront of your mind. Begin each day with a morning intention-setting ritual. As you wake, take a few moments to center yourself, breathing deeply and calmly. Visualize your intention clearly and vividly, feeling the emotions associated with its realization. This practice sets a positive tone for the day, priming your mind and spirit to pursue your goals with determination and focus. Journaling is another effective method for harnessing the power of intentions. Write down your intentions, detailing the steps you will take to achieve them, and regularly review your progress. This practice not only clarifies your goals but also tracks your journey, providing insight into your growth and development.

Tracking and reflecting on your intentions is vital for understanding their impact and adjusting your approach as needed. An intention journal serves as a valuable tool for this purpose. Record your intentions, along with any observations or experiences related to them. Note any challenges or obstacles you encounter, and consider how they might influence your path. Periodically, engage in monthly reflection rituals to assess your progress. Set aside time to review your journal entries, contemplating the lessons learned and the changes required to stay aligned with your goals. This reflective practice fosters awareness and adaptability, enabling you to refine your intentions and strategies for greater success.

## 7.3 Enhancing Psychic Defense Mechanisms

When you walk through a dense forest, or a dark ally the path ahead can be shrouded in mist. Your senses are heightened, every rustle of leaves and snap of twigs alerting you to potential threats lurking in the shadows. This is akin to navigating the unseen world of psychic energies, where threats are not always visible but can be deeply felt. Psychic defense mechanisms serve as your shield against these intangible forces. They are protective strategies that guard your energy field from negative influences, much like armor that deflects unseen arrows. Understanding these defenses is paramount for maintaining your psychic health, ensuring that you remain grounded and resilient in the face of life's challenges.

Psychic threats can manifest in various forms, from emotional vampires who drain your energy to environments thick with negativity that leave you feeling depleted. The importance of psychic health cannot be overstated. Just as you care for your physical body, your psychic well-being requires attention and upkeep. When neglected, psychic vulnerabilities can lead to feelings of anxiety, depression, and fatigue. By bolstering your defenses, you empower yourself to navigate the world with confidence and clarity, secure in the knowledge that your energy is protected and sustained.

Developing psychic awareness is the first step in fortifying these defenses. It involves tuning into the subtle energies around you, enhancing your ability to detect and counteract psychic attacks. Meditation is a powerful tool for this purpose. Quiet the mind and focusing inward, you will heighten your perception, becoming more attuned to the energetic shifts in your environment. Through regular meditation practice, you cultivate a deep sense of presence and awareness, enabling you to discern the nuances of psychic influences more clearly. Additionally, exercises designed to strengthen psychic sensitivity can further enhance your awareness. These might include practices like energy scanning, where you consciously move your awareness through your body to identify areas of tension or imbalance. Such exercises not only deepen your connection to your own energy field but also improve your ability to perceive external energies, equipping you with the insight needed to protect against unwanted intrusions.

Once you have honed your awareness, building psychic shields becomes your next line of defense. These shields are energetic barriers that protect you from external negative influences, much like a protective bubble that surrounds and safeguards your aura. Visualization techniques are key in creating these shields. Begin by envisioning a radiant light enveloping you, forming an impenetrable barrier that deflects negativity and harm. This light can take any color or form that resonates with you, whether it's a shimmering sphere or a cloak of golden energy. As you visualize, infuse this shield with your intention for protection, reinforcing its strength and durability. The use of protective crystals and stones can further enhance your shield's effectiveness. Stones like black tourmaline or obsidian have grounding and protective properties, absorbing negative energies and preventing them from penetrating your field. Carry these stones with you or place them in your environment to bolster your defenses and maintain a sanctuary of positive energy.

Maintaining psychic health is an ongoing practice, requiring regular cleansing and balancing rituals to ensure your energy remains vibrant and resilient. These rituals can be simple yet effective, incorporating elements like water, sound, or sage to cleanse and restore your aura. Regularly engage in activities like smudging with sage or bathing in saltwater to wash away accumulated negativity, leaving your energy field refreshed and renewed. Balancing rituals, such as chakra alignment meditations, help to harmonize your internal energy centers, promoting a sense of equilibrium and well-being. By dedicating time to these practices, you cultivate a sustainable state of psychic health, empowering you to face life's challenges with a fortified spirit and unwavering confidence.

***

## 7.4 Empowerment Through Historical Witchcraft Practices

Imagine stepping into an age-old library, the air thick with the scent of parchment and candle wax. As you pull ancient spellbooks and grimoires from the dusty shelves, you are not just reading words. You're connecting with the very essence of those who came before you. These texts, filled with rituals and incantations, served as guides for countless practitioners seeking empowerment through the ages. They held the secrets of healing, protection, and transformation, passed down through generations. The study of these ancient texts reveals a rich tapestry of traditions, each one offering insights into the use of natural elements and the power of intention. From the herbal concoctions of the wise women of the Middle Ages to the astrological charts of Renaissance magicians, these practices remind us of the enduring connection between humans and the natural world.

Adapting these historical practices for modern use involves honoring their origins while allowing room for innovation. Today's world is vastly different from the one in which these rituals were first practiced, yet their essence remains relevant. Modern practitioners can draw inspiration from these old-world rituals, integrating them with contemporary tools and materials. For instance, the use of digital technology can enhance traditional practices by providing new ways to track lunar phases or share ritual experiences with a global community. Similarly, incorporating modern materials like essential oils or crystals into age-old spellwork can add a new dimension, making the rituals feel both ancient and immediate. In this way, the past and present blend seamlessly, creating a practice that is robust and adaptable.

Throughout history, certain figures stand out for their contributions to the practice and empowerment of witchcraft. Figures like Gerald Gardner, who is often credited with popularizing modern Wicca, and Doreen Valiente, known for her work in crafting many foundational Wiccan texts, have left legacies that continue to inspire practitioners today. Their lives and works exemplify how witchcraft can be a means of personal empowerment and spiritual growth. By studying their techniques and philosophies, we can gain insights into how they harnessed the forces of nature and spirit to create change in their lives and the lives of others. Their stories are not just about magic but about resilience, creativity, and the courage to challenge societal norms.

Incorporating ancestral wisdom into your personal practice is a powerful way to honor those who have paved the path before you. Ancestral spirits, whether they are known to you or not, offer guidance and support, connecting you to a lineage of knowledge and tradition. Honoring these spirits in your rituals can be as simple as lighting a candle in their memory or as elaborate as creating a sacred altar space adorned with offerings and symbols of their presence. Drawing inspiration from your cultural heritage can also enrich your practice, providing a deeper understanding of your roots and the unique gifts they bring. Whether through the revival of family traditions or the exploration of cultural myths and legends, embracing this heritage allows you to walk your path with the strength and wisdom of those who came before.

In this exploration of historical witchcraft practices, you find a wellspring of empowerment. The past offers a rich source of knowledge, waiting to be rediscovered and reimagined for today's world. By embracing these ancient techniques, adapting them with modern insights, and honoring the wisdom of historical figures and ancestral spirits, you create a practice that is both deeply personal and universally connected. This approach not only empowers you as a practitioner but also honors the legacy of those who have used these practices to find strength, healing, and transformation throughout the ages. Every spell, every ritual, becomes a thread in the tapestry of history, a testament to the enduring power of witchcraft as a tool for empowerment and change.

## 7.5 Psychological Tactics for Empowerment

Understanding oneself can be a powerful tool for empowerment, a way to navigate life's complexities with confidence and clarity. It starts with introspection, a deep dive into your thoughts, emotions, and motivations. Techniques like journaling and meditation can aid in this process. Through regular journaling, you record your thoughts and feelings, creating a map of your inner world. This practice not only highlights recurring patterns but also uncovers hidden strengths and weaknesses. Meditation, on the other hand, quiets the mind, allowing for self-reflection without judgment. It is in these moments of stillness that insights often emerge, providing clarity about what truly matters and where your passions lie. These tools help identify personal strengths, the unique qualities that set you apart. Recognizing these strengths is the first step in using them to your advantage, empowering you to face challenges with poise and resilience.

Building confidence and self-efficacy—the belief in your ability to succeed—is not just about skill but mindset. Visualization is a potent technique in this regard. Picture yourself achieving your goals, every detail vivid and real. How do you feel? What are you doing? This exercise trains the mind to anticipate success, making it a familiar destination. Overcoming self-doubt, a common barrier, requires a shift in perception. Start by challenging negative self-talk. Replace "I can't" with "I can" and observe the difference it makes. Affirmations, simple yet effective, reinforce this shift. Repeating statements like "I am capable" or "I am worthy" rewires the brain to think positively. As you internalize these affirmations, they become part of your belief system, fortifying your confidence from within.

Positive reinforcement is another key strategy in fostering empowering behaviors. It involves acknowledging and celebrating achievements, no matter how small. By setting up a reward system, you create a cycle of motivation. Each accomplishment, whether completing a task or reaching a goal, triggers a reward. This could be as simple as taking a moment to savor a cup of coffee or treating yourself to something special. The act of rewarding reinforces positive actions, encouraging repetition and creating a habit of success. Over time, this approach builds a foundation of achievement that boosts self-esteem and confidence, making empowerment a natural state of being.

Implementing behavioral change involves adopting new habits and mindsets that align with your goals. Habit formation is a gradual process, one that begins with small, manageable steps. Identify a behavior you wish to change or adopt, and break it down into achievable actions. Consistency is key, as repeated actions become ingrained over time. Goal-setting frameworks, such as SMART (Specific, Measurable, Achievable, Relevant, Time-bound), provide structure and clarity. By setting specific and realistic goals, you create a roadmap for success. Regularly review and adjust your goals, celebrating milestones along the way. This practice not only keeps you focused but also adaptable, ensuring that your path to empowerment is dynamic and responsive to change. Through these psychological tactics, empowerment becomes not just a goal, but a way of life, a continuous journey of self-discovery and growth.

## 7.6 Rituals for Manifesting Personal Goals

Setting personal goals is a powerful act, akin to planting seeds that will one day grow into a bountiful harvest. Rituals serve as the fertile soil, nurturing these seeds and providing the structure needed for growth. By engaging in goal-setting ceremonies, you create a sacred space where your intentions are clearly defined and energetically charged. This process can involve gathering symbolic representations of your goals—objects, images, or words that embody your aspirations. For example, if your goal is to achieve financial stability, you might include coins or images of prosperity. These symbols act as tangible manifestations of your desires, grounding your intentions in the physical world and aligning your subconscious mind with your conscious aims.

Manifesting your goals through ritual practice taps into the power of visualization and affirmation. Visualization rituals involve closing your eyes and vividly imagining the successful achievement of your goals. Picture every detail: the sights, sounds, and emotions that accompany your success. This mental rehearsal imprints the desired outcome onto your subconscious, making it feel both achievable and inevitable. Affirmation rituals, on the other hand, involve verbalizing your goals as if they have already been accomplished. Speak statements like "I am thriving in my new career" or "I have achieved a balanced lifestyle." The repetition of these affirmations reinforces belief and commitment, turning what once seemed distant into a present reality. Manifestation jars or boxes can also enhance this process. By placing written goals or symbolic items inside, you create a physical representation of your aspirations. Each time you add to or interact with the jar, you reinforce your commitment and connection to your goals.

Tracking progress toward your goals is important to maintain momentum and making necessary adjustments. Rituals for acknowledging milestones provide an opportunity to reflect on achievements and recalibrate your efforts. As you reach significant milestones, take time to celebrate and recognize your progress. This could be as simple as lighting a candle in gratitude or creating a small altar dedicated to each accomplishment. Reflective practices, such as journaling or meditative contemplation, help you realign your strategies and intentions, ensuring that your path remains clear and focused. Through these practices, you gain insight into what works well and what might need modification, allowing you to adapt with grace and agility.

Celebrating achievements through ritual not only reinforces goal attainment but also infuses your journey with joy and gratitude. Celebration ceremonies can be tailored to suit your preferences, whether it's a quiet moment of reflection or a lively gathering with friends. These rituals acknowledge the effort and dedication required to achieve your goals, providing a sense of closure and fulfillment. Incorporating gratitude practices further enhances this experience, shifting your focus from what you have yet to accomplish to the abundance you have already created. Gratitude journaling, where you list things you're thankful for, fosters a mindset of positivity and appreciation, attracting even more success and fulfillment into your life.

As you integrate these rituals into your life, they become more than mere practices—they are pathways to empowerment and transformation. Each ritual serves as a stepping stone, guiding you toward your goals while deepening your connection to your inner self. Through the intentional use of rituals, you harness the power of intention and manifestation, aligning your actions with your deepest desires. These practices support your personal growth and also contribute to a life rich with purpose and meaning. In this way, rituals for manifesting personal goals are not just tools for achievement but also expressions of your unique journey through life.

# Connecting with Supportive Communities

Historically, covens provided witches with a space to meet, support each other, exchange knowledge, and avoid conflict. Today, many white witches prefer solitude due to busy work schedules or long distances to gatherings. However, they utilize digital platforms to connect with like-minded individuals. As humans, we are naturally inclined to seek connection. Today, online covens and Wicca communities offer opportunities to engage with others. Take the time to educate yourself and choose the path that aligns best with your beliefs and needs.

## 8.1 Find your Tribe

Finding your tribe involves identifying communities that resonate with your interests and values, offering a sense of belonging and understanding. Begin by exploring local workshops and events where practitioners and enthusiasts gather to share knowledge and experiences. These gatherings provide a fertile ground for connection, allowing you to engage with others who share your path. Whether it's a workshop on herbal remedies or a lecture on psychological resilience, these events offer insights and inspiration. Participating in online and offline niche discussion forums broadens your horizons, exposing you to diverse perspectives and practices. These forums act as virtual gathering spaces where conversations flow freely, and ideas are exchanged. Here, you can find your voice, contribute to discussions, and learn from others, fostering a sense of community and collaboration.

***

Building meaningful connections within these communities requires a proactive approach, where networking becomes a tool for growth and support. Attending conferences and gatherings can open doors to new relationships as you meet individuals who share your passion and curiosity. These events are not just about learning but also about forming bonds that extend beyond the sessions. Engaging in collaborative projects offers another avenue for connection, allowing you to work alongside others on shared goals. Whether it's co-creating a ritual or researching a topic of mutual interest, collaboration fosters deeper ties and mutual respect.

Joining study groups or book clubs can further enrich your experience, providing regular opportunities for discussion and exploration. These gatherings become spaces of learning and camaraderie, where ideas are discussed and friendships blossom.

Sometimes, the community you seek doesn't yet exist, and you might feel called to create your own gathering of like-minded souls. Setting up local meetups or online groups allows you to curate a space that reflects your interests and values. Consider hosting community events or rituals and inviting others to join in shared practices and celebrations. These events can be as simple or elaborate as you choose, from a casual coffee chat to a full moon gathering. The key is to create an environment that welcomes diversity and fosters inclusion, where everyone feels valued and heard. As the community grows, you'll find that the connections formed become a source of strength and inspiration, enriching your journey and those of others who join you.

Sustaining engagement within these communities requires ongoing effort and commitment, ensuring that connections remain vibrant and meaningful. Regular communication is essential, whether through newsletters that keep members informed or group chats that spark lively discussions. This consistent interaction maintains a sense of continuity, encouraging active participation and involvement. Organizing recurring events or study sessions provides structure and routine, offering members something to look forward to and engage with. These gatherings become touchstones in the community calendar, anchoring the group and reinforcing the bonds that hold it together. By fostering a culture of openness and collaboration, you ensure that the community remains dynamic and inclusive, a place where everyone can contribute and thrive.

> Interactive Element: Community-Building Exercise
> Think about what interests or values are most important to you. Write a list of five potential community activities or events you'd like to participate in or create. Consider how you might find or build a community around these interests. Reflect on what steps you can take to engage with others and sustain these connections.

## 8.2 Online Spaces for Witchcraft Enthusiasts

In the digital age, the search for like-minded individuals often begins online, where a multitude of spaces dedicated to witchcraft await. These virtual communities are as diverse as the practices they encompass, offering something for everyone, whether you're a seasoned practitioner or a curious newcomer. Social media groups and pages serve as vibrant hubs for sharing ideas, asking questions, and finding inspiration. Platforms like Facebook and Instagram boast numerous groups focused on everything from herbal magic to lunar rituals, each with its own flavor and community vibe. These spaces invite you to engage with others who share your interests, fostering a sense of connection and belonging.

Dedicated online forums and websites provide deeper dives into the multifaceted world of witchcraft. Here, you can find discussions on niche topics, from crystal healing to shadow work, offering a wealth of information and perspectives. Websites often host a variety of resources, including articles, tutorials, and member blogs, which contribute to a rich tapestry of knowledge and practice. These forums offer a more structured environment for learning and interaction, where members can engage in thoughtful discussions and exchange insights with practitioners from around the globe. The diversity of these online spaces reflects the inclusivity of modern witchcraft, welcoming individuals from all walks of life to explore and grow together.

Participating in virtual events has become an invaluable way to enhance learning and connection within the online witchcraft community. Webinars and online workshops provide opportunities to learn from experienced practitioners and experts in the field. These events often cover a wide range of topics, from introductory spells to advanced techniques, allowing you to tailor your learning experience to your interests and skill level. Virtual ritual gatherings, too, offer a unique experience, bringing people together to participate in shared practices despite physical distances. These gatherings foster a sense of unity and collective energy, reinforcing the bonds within the community and offering an opportunity to witness and participate in diverse rituals and traditions.

Building an online presence within the witchcraft community is both rewarding and empowering, offering a platform to share your journey, insights, and experiences. Creating a blog or YouTube channel allows you to express your unique perspective and connect with others who resonate with your message. These platforms provide a space to document your practices, share your knowledge, and engage in dialogue with a broader audience. Engaging with followers on social media platforms further enhances your presence, offering real-time interactions and the opportunity to build relationships with like-minded individuals. This engagement not only fosters community but also contributes to your personal growth, as you learn and evolve alongside others.

Ensuring safety and privacy while engaging in online communities is paramount, protecting both your personal information and your sense of security. Using pseudonyms or avatars can help maintain anonymity, allowing you to participate freely without revealing your identity. This practice is especially important if you wish to explore sensitive topics or share personal experiences without fear of judgment or exposure. Being cautious with personal information is equally crucial, as online platforms can be vulnerable to breaches or misuse. Avoid sharing details such as your address, phone number, or financial information, and consider using secure communication methods for private conversations. By taking these precautions, you can enjoy the benefits of online community participation while safeguarding your privacy.

The digital landscape offers a rich and varied environment for exploring witchcraft, connecting with others, and expanding your knowledge and practice. Whether you're browsing a forum, attending a virtual workshop, or sharing your insights on a blog, the opportunities for growth and connection are endless. Embrace the diversity and inclusivity of these online spaces, and you'll find a supportive community ready to welcome you with open arms.

***

## 8.3 Safe Spaces for Discussing Dark Psychology

Creating a safe space for discussing dark psychology starts with clear intentions and a commitment to confidentiality and respect. It's about constructing an environment where everyone can feel secure to express thoughts and explore sensitive subjects without fear of judgment or exposure. Establishing ground rules is paramount, setting the tone for interactions. These might include guidelines about respecting diverse perspectives, maintaining confidentiality, and fostering an atmosphere of empathy. Such rules create a foundation of trust, allowing participants to engage openly and honestly. Confidentiality is the cornerstone of these spaces, ensuring that what is shared remains protected, fostering a sense of security and openness. Respect, too, is vital, as it acknowledges the value of each person's contributions and experiences, reinforcing the importance of dignity and understanding in these discussions.

Facilitating open dialogue within these safe spaces requires a delicate balance of encouragement and moderation. Encouraging respectful debate invites participants to explore differing viewpoints, fostering a richer understanding of dark psychology's complexities. This dialogue should be guided by empathy, where questions are posed not to challenge but to understand. Providing resources for further exploration can deepen these discussions, offering participants avenues to expand their knowledge and insights. These resources might include recommended readings, documentaries, or expert talks, which enrich the conversation and provide context. The goal is to create a dynamic environment where learning is reciprocal, and every participant feels empowered to both teach and learn. Open dialogue thrives when participants feel heard and valued, encouraging a culture of inclusivity and curiosity.

Finding supportive networks is fundamental for anyone looking to explore the complexities of dark psychology. Professional organizations and associations offer structured environments where knowledge is shared and developed. These groups often host events and discussions, providing platforms for individuals to connect with experts and peers alike. Peer support groups and mentorship programs offer more intimate settings, where individuals can share experiences and seek guidance from those who have walked similar paths. These networks provide not only knowledge but also a sense of belonging, where everyone can feel understood and supported. The connections made within these groups can be eye-opening, offering both personal and professional growth. Supportive networks are important for anyone exploring the complexities of dark psychology, providing a community that understands and shares their journey.

Handling sensitive topics with care and empathy is a skill that requires awareness and intention. Recognizing and respecting triggers is a fundamental aspect as it acknowledges the personal and emotional impact of certain topics. This sensitivity can be fostered by encouraging participants to share any topics they find challenging, allowing facilitators to navigate discussions with care. Providing content warnings or disclaimers before diving into potentially distressing material is another profound strategy. These warnings prepare participants, giving them the choice to engage or step back if needed. Empathy is the key to handling sensitive discussions, as it invites understanding and connection. By approaching these topics with compassion and care, facilitators can create a space where individuals feel safe to explore and express their perspectives. This approach not only respects individual boundaries but also fosters a deeper, more meaningful dialogue.

> Reflective Exercise: Establishing Personal Boundaries in Discussions
>
> Consider what boundaries you need to feel safe when discussing sensitive topics. Reflect on past experiences where discussions felt either supportive or challenging. Write down three strategies you can use to establish these boundaries in future discussions. This reflection will help you identify what you need to feel secure and respected, ensuring that you can engage in meaningful dialogue without compromising your well-being.

***

## 8.4 Sharing Rituals: Group Practices

Group rituals possess an energy that can be transformative, amplifying the power of individual intentions through collective focus. Participating in these shared practices allows each participant to contribute their energy, creating a synergy that enhances the overall experience. This collective energy not only strengthens the ritual's impact but also fosters a profound sense of belonging. In these moments, you are not just practicing magic; you are part of a community, connected by shared purpose and understanding. The bonds formed in these circles often extend beyond the ritual itself, creating lasting friendships and a supportive network of like-minded individuals.

Designing group rituals requires thoughtful collaboration, where ideas and intentions are woven together to create a cohesive and powerful experience. Start by gathering with your group to discuss themes and elements that resonate with everyone involved. This collaborative process ensures that each participant feels invested and valued, contributing their unique perspectives and insights. Once a theme is established, assign roles and responsibilities to ensure a smooth and organized ceremony. Some may take on the role of the facilitator, guiding the ritual's flow, while others might focus on specific elements like music, offerings, or altar arrangements. By distributing responsibilities, you allow each member to engage fully, bringing their strengths to the fore. This shared ownership enriches the ritual, as each participant's energy and intention are integral to its success.

Inclusivity is a cornerstone of group rituals, ensuring that everyone can participate fully and meaningfully. Consider the diverse backgrounds and abilities of your group, adapting rituals to accommodate varying needs and preferences.

This might involve incorporating practices from different cultural traditions, honoring the richness of each participant's heritage. Additionally, be mindful of physical abilities, adapting movements or positions to ensure everyone is comfortable and included. For instance, if a ritual involves standing or moving, offer alternatives for those who may find these actions challenging. This commitment to inclusivity fosters a sense of safety and respect, encouraging open and authentic participation. By creating an environment where everyone feels welcome, you strengthen the community bonds that are so vital to the ritual's success.

Celebrating seasonal and cultural events through group rituals offers a wonderful opportunity to connect with the rhythms of nature and the diverse traditions of your community. Organizing gatherings for solstices, equinoxes, or other significant cultural events can bring the community together in meaningful ways. These celebrations provide a chance to honor the cycles of the year, aligning your practices with the natural world. Incorporating cultural traditions and practices adds depth and richness to these gatherings, offering a space for learning and sharing. Encourage participants to bring elements from their cultural backgrounds, whether through songs, dances, or symbols. This exchange of traditions not only enriches the ritual but also fosters a deeper understanding and appreciation of each other's heritage. By celebrating these events together, you create a tapestry of shared experiences that strengthens the community and nurtures the spirit.

In the heart of a group ritual lies an alchemy of connection, where individual people come together to create something greater than the sum of their parts. The shared energy and focus transform the ritual into a powerful act of unity and intention. Whether you are designing a new ritual or adapting an existing one, the emphasis on collaboration, inclusivity, and celebration ensures that each gathering is a meaningful and enriching experience. Through these practices, you build a community that supports and uplifts each member, reinforcing the bonds that make shared rituals such a profound and transformative experience.

## 8.5 Ethical Leadership in Community Building

In community building, particularly within the complex worlds of witchcraft and dark psychology, ethical leadership is key. It's grounded in transparency and honesty, where leaders openly share clear and truthful information with their communities, cultivating trust and empowerment. Transparency ensures that members feel informed and confident in their leaders' intentions. Equally important is accountability—leaders must take responsibility for their decisions and actions, whether the outcomes are good or bad. By demonstrating integrity and leading by example, they inspire others to follow suit, fostering a culture of trust and responsibility.

Building trust and respect within a community takes intentional effort and a commitment to open communication. Encouraging feedback from members brings in diverse perspectives, fueling growth and development. When members feel safe to voice concerns, share ideas, and offer suggestions without fear of judgment, it creates a culture of openness. Leaders who actively listen and respond to this feedback foster a sense of belonging and mutual respect, strengthening the community's unity. Leading by example is equally impactful—when leaders model ethical behavior and embody the values they promote, they inspire confidence and trust. This alignment between actions and words reinforces bonds and sets the tone for a strong, cohesive community.

Conflicts and challenges are inevitable in any community, but effective management can transform these into opportunities for growth and understanding. Mediation and conflict resolution techniques provide structured approaches to navigate disagreements, focusing on finding common ground and mutual understanding. These techniques encourage open dialogue, where each party's perspective is heard and validated. Establishing clear protocols and procedures for addressing conflicts ensures that issues are handled consistently and fairly, reducing the potential for misunderstandings and resentment. By addressing conflicts with empathy and respect, leaders can turn challenges into learning experiences, reinforcing the community's resilience and unity.

Promoting growth and development within a community is a key responsibility of ethical leadership. Providing opportunities for skill development empowers members to expand their knowledge and capabilities, enriching both their personal journeys and the community as a whole. Workshops, seminars, and training sessions offer valuable platforms for learning and exploration, encouraging members to pursue their interests and passions. Encouraging continuous learning fosters a culture of curiosity and innovation, where members are inspired to explore new ideas and perspectives. This commitment to growth not only enhances individual potential but also strengthens the community's collective wisdom and adaptability. As leaders nurture an environment of learning and development, they cultivate a vibrant, dynamic community that thrives on diversity and collaboration.

***

In essence, ethical leadership within witchcraft and dark psychology communities is about fostering an environment where transparency, accountability, and respect are paramount. By cultivating these values, leaders create spaces where trust can flourish, conflicts can be navigated with grace, and members can grow and develop to their fullest potential. This approach not only strengthens the community's foundation but also empowers its members to contribute meaningfully to the shared vision and goals. Through ethical leadership, communities become more than just gatherings of individuals; they transform into supportive networks where each member is valued, heard, and inspired to thrive.

***

## 8.6 Navigating Social Judgment and Stigma

The legacy of fear and misunderstanding continues to shape how witchcraft and dark psychology are perceived. For centuries, persecution and stigma cast practitioners as sinister outsiders, rooted in the witch hunts and demonization of those who challenged mainstream beliefs. Even today, modern portrayals often oversimplify or sensationalize these practices, perpetuating harmful stereotypes. Witchcraft is frequently reduced to being either whimsical or sinister, while dark psychology is viewed as purely manipulative and unethical. These misconceptions create barriers, fostering judgment and criticism, and leaving practitioners to navigate a world still influenced by prejudice and misinformation.

Building resilience against social judgment is crucial for anyone walking these paths. It starts with developing a strong sense of self-worth, a foundation that remains unshaken by external opinions. Embrace your identity with pride, recognizing the value and authenticity of your practices. Self-care plays a vital role here, acting as a buffer against negativity. Engage in activities that nurture your spirit and reinforce your sense of self, whether through meditation, journaling, or simply spending time in nature. Self-compassion, too, is essential; treating yourself with kindness and understanding helps mitigate the impact of criticism. Acknowledge your feelings without judgment, allowing yourself the grace to process and heal. By cultivating these internal strengths, you can withstand external pressures with resilience and confidence, remaining true to your beliefs and values.

***

Advocacy and education are powerful tools for challenging societal misconceptions and fostering understanding. Engaging in public awareness campaigns can illuminate the truths behind witchcraft and dark psychology, dispelling myths and encouraging open dialogue. These campaigns might involve writing articles, hosting workshops, or speaking at events to share accurate information and personal insights. Sharing your own stories and experiences can also make a significant impact, offering a human face to practices often shrouded in mystery. Personal narratives have the power to connect with others on an emotional level, breaking down barriers and fostering empathy. By stepping into the role of educator, you contribute to a broader cultural shift, one that embraces diversity and encourages curiosity over judgment. Having said this – please consider to not over-share your experiences – in a world of doubt it can be hard to keep your confidence and positive attitude against a barrage of negativity.

Creating allies and support networks is an essential strategy for combating stigma. Partnering with like-minded organizations can amplify your voice, providing a platform for collective advocacy and education. These partnerships offer resources and support, creating a united front that challenges stereotypes and promotes acceptance. Building relationships with supportive individuals further strengthens your resilience, offering a network of encouragement and understanding. These allies provide a safe space for expression and exploration, where you can share experiences without fear of judgment. Together, these connections form a community of support, fostering a sense of belonging and empowerment. Through collaboration and mutual support, you can navigate the challenges of social stigma with strength and solidarity.

As you integrate these strategies into your life, you cultivate an environment where you can thrive, free from the constraints of judgment and misconception. The strength you build within yourself and the connections you forge with others lay the groundwork for a future where understanding and acceptance prevail. With resilience, advocacy, and community, you can transform societal perceptions, paving the way for acceptance and appreciation of diverse practices. This shift not only enriches your personal journey but also contributes to a broader cultural evolution, where diversity is celebrated and all paths are honored.

# Conclusion

As we draw this journey to a close, it's time to revisit the core concepts that have guided our exploration. At the heart of our discussion is the fusion of white witchcraft and dark psychology.

We explored the essence of white witchcraft, an ancient practice focused on channeling positive energy for healing and protection. Its rich history has been a source of empowerment for many, offering tools and rituals that nurture the spirit and safeguard against harm.

On the other side, dark psychology uncovers manipulation tactics that exploit vulnerabilities, shedding light on the pervasive influence of such practices in modern society. By understanding both, you gain a balanced perspective that empowers you to safely live in a world where these forces often intermingle.

Throughout this book, each chapter has been a stepping stone towards understanding and integration. We've examined how ancient magical practices intersect with contemporary psychology, offering dual solutions that are both mystical and practical. From identifying energy vampires in your life to creating protective sigils, each chapter provided strategies to enhance your personal power and protection. We explored rituals that cleanse and protect, alongside psychological defenses that bolster your mental resilience. The journey also took us through ethical considerations, emphasizing the importance of intent and responsibility in all practices.

Key takeaways from our exploration include the critical role of self-awareness and the power of rituals in safeguarding your well-being. Understanding manipulation tactics and setting boundaries are ground breaking skills in a world where control is often subtle yet pervasive. Moreover, the ethical implications of wielding such knowledge cannot be overstated. Respecting free will and practicing with integrity ensures that your actions remain aligned with your values. By integrating these lessons, you protect yourself and foster a life of empowerment and authenticity.

Reflect on the insights gained, and consider how they might transform your approach to self-protection and personal empowerment. The knowledge you've acquired is not just theoretical but practical, intended to be used in your daily life. Whether it's through morning rituals that set your intentions or through mindfulness practices that keep you grounded, these tools are yours to shape your reality.

*** 

<u>Now, it's time for action. I encourage you to apply what you've learned.</u> Implement daily rituals that resonate with you and practice the psychological defense strategies discussed. Engage with communities that support your growth and exploration. By doing so, you create a network of support and strength, reinforcing the foundations you've built throughout this book.

The journey doesn't end here. Continue to explore witchcraft and psychology. Seek out further reading, join discussions, and experiment with new techniques. The world of knowledge is vast, and every new discovery enriches your understanding and practice. Embrace the curiosity that led you here and let it guide you further.

This book's vision is to empower you to protect yourself against manipulation and enhance your life through the fusion of ancient wisdom and modern insights. The path you choose is uniquely yours, crafted by your choices and the knowledge you wield. By merging these elements, you're equipped to face the challenges ahead with confidence and clarity.

As you close this chapter, carry with you an empowering message: you possess the tools to create a life defined by empowerment, protection, and integrity. The knowledge and strategies you've gained are not just for defense but for nurturing the life you desire. Embrace them, trust in your journey, and move forward with the assurance that you are capable of transforming challenges into opportunities. The power lies within you, waiting to be harnessed and expressed in your unique way.

# A Note from Selena

## HELP OTHERS BY SHARING YOUR THOUGHTS

Hi there, lovely reader!

Thank you for spending time with *White Witchcraft vs Dark Psychology*. Writing this book was a deeply personal journey, and knowing you're here, exploring these pages, means so much to me.

If this book has sparked any thoughts, feelings, or insights for you, I'd be honored if you could take a moment to share them in a review. Your voice has the power to inspire others to embark on their own journey with this book.

It doesn't have to be long or formal—just a few words about what stood out to you or how it makes you feel. Reviews not only help other readers but also bring me incredible joy and motivation as a writer.

Thank you for being part of this adventure with me. Wishing you light, clarity! Blessed Be as you continue your journey!

With gratitude,
Selena

# References

## References

- *White magic* https://en.wikipedia.org/wiki/White_magic

- *Sigmund Freud's Life, Theories, and Influence - Verywell Mind* https://www.verywellmind.com/sigmund-freud-his-life-work-and-theories-2795860#:~:text=Sigmund%20Freud's%20theories%20and%20work,in%20opposition%20to%20his%20ideas.

- *How Witches Evolved from Social Outcasts to Pop-Culture ...* https://now.tufts.edu/2024/10/09/how-witches-evolved-social-outcasts-pop-culture-heroines

- *Ethical principles of psychologists and code of conduct* https://www.apa.org/ethics/code

- *Energy Vampires: 10 Signs to Watch For and How to Deal ...* https://www.healthline.com/health/mental-health/energy-vampires

- *6 brilliant ways to cleanse your aura and invite good*

*energies* https://timesofindia.indiatimes.com/life-style/soul-search/6-brilliant-ways-to-cleanse-your-aura-and-invite-good-energies/photostory/110455680.cms

- *Defense Mechanisms In Psychology Explained (+ Examples)* https://www.simplypsychology.org/defense-mechanisms.html

- *Manipulation in Relationships: Signs, Behaviors, & How to ...* https://www.verywellmind.com/manipulation-in-marriage-2302245

- *Magical Grounding, Centering, and Shielding Techniques* https://www.learnreligions.com/grounding-centering-and-shielding-4122187

- *Shadow Work: A 3-Part Guide for Integrating Your Dark Side* https://scottjeffrey.com/shadow-work/

- *Effects of Mindfulness on Psychological Health: A Review ...* https://pmc.ncbi.nlm.nih.gov/articles/PMC3679190/

- *Protection Magick: Why And How It Is Useful In Everyday Life* https://www.patheos.com/blogs/3pagansandacat/2020/05/protection-spells-why-and-how-it-is-useful-in-everyday-life/

- *Healing myself the Pagan way: how witchcraft cast a spell ...* https://www.theguardian.com/lifeandstyle/2021/dec/26/healing-myself-the-pagan-way-how-witchcraft-cast-a-spell-on-me

- *The 7 Stages of Emotional Healing: A Roadmap to Peace* https://www.growingself.com/seven-stages-of-emotional-healing/

- *Cleansing In Modern Paganism And Witchcraft | John Beckett* https://www.patheos.com/blogs/johnbeckett/2023/02/cleansing-in-modern-paganism-and-witchcraft.html

- *Forgiveness: Letting go of grudges and bitterness - Mayo Clinic* https://www.mayoclinic.org/healthy-lifestyle/adult-health/in-depth/forgiveness/art-20047692#:~:text=The%20act%20that%20hurt%20or,the%20one%20who%20hurt%20you.

- *Embracing Modern Witchcraft: A Journey of Magic and ...* https://www.downtowntarot.com/post/embracing-modern-witchcraft-a-journey-of-magic-and-community

- *The Dark Side of Psychological Safety: Sometimes You Are ...* https://interactiveworkshops.com/the-dark-side-of-psychological-safety-sometimes-you-are-not-supposed-to-feel-safe-at-work/

- *Online Witchcraft Community. Focus on Resources* https://digitaloccultlibrary.commons.gc.cuny.edu/forums/topic/online-witchcraft-community-focus-on-resources/

- *Spiritual values and practices related to leadership ...* https://www.sciencedirect.com/science/article/ab

s/pii/S1048984305000718

- *The Morality of Hexing and Cursing* https://bryjaimea.com/witchcraft/ethics-and-explorations/the-morality-of-hexing-and-cursing/

- *Consent vs. Disregard of Boundaries* https://www.psychologytoday.com/intl/blog/you-cant-sit-with-us/201905/consent-vs-disregard-of-boundaries

- *Harm Reduction Principles* https://harmreduction.org/about-us/principles-of-harm-reduction/

- *The mummy's curse: historical cohort study - PMC* https://pmc.ncbi.nlm.nih.gov/articles/PMC139048/

- *Salem and Seneca: The Rise of Witchcraft and Women's ...* https://www.therutgersreview.com/2020/10/28/salem-and-seneca-the-rise-of-witchcraft-and-womens-empowerment/

- *Advanced sigil magic techniques? : r/chaosmagick* https://www.reddit.com/r/chaosmagick/comments/mqgv7p/advanced_sigil_magic_techniques/

- *10 Transformational Empowerment Strategies for Life and ...* https://www.psychologytoday.com/us/blog/flourish-and-thrive/202205/10-transformational-empowerment-strategies-for-life-and-work

- *6 Rituals For Manifestation That Energy Workers Swear By* https://www.bustle.com/life/manifestation-rituals-energy-workers

- *BBC Radio 4 - Nine extraordinary facts about British witchcraft* https://www.bbc.co.uk/programmes/articles/4k9wKxypN25pfyXv4k0lbks/nine-extraordinary-facts-about-british-witchcraft#:~:text=Witches%20used%20to%20be%20a,as%20remedies%20for%20various%20ailments.

- *The Power of Rituals in Personal Development* https://medium.com/@godwinakpe3/the-power-of-rituals-in-personal-development-03c2b4b869b3

- *Psychological Benefits of Routines - Mental Health* https://www.webmd.com/mental-health/psychological-benefits-of-routine

- *How to Develop Emotional Intelligence Skills - HBS Online* https://online.hbs.edu/blog/post/emotional-intelligence-skills

www.ingramcontent.com/pod-product-compliance
Lightning Source LLC
Chambersburg PA
CBHW060612080526
44585CB00013B/799